Is the Last Mile the Longest? Economic Gains from Gender Equality in Nordic Countries

This work is published under the responsibility of the Secretary-General of the OECD. The opinions expressed and arguments employed herein do not necessarily reflect the official views of OECD member countries.

This document, as well as any data and any map included herein, are without prejudice to the status of or sovereignty over any territory, to the delimitation of international frontiers and boundaries and to the name of any territory, city or area.

Please cite this publication as:
OECD (2018), *Is the Last Mile the Longest? Economic Gains from Gender Equality in Nordic Countries*, OECD Publishing, Paris.
http://dx.doi.org/10.1787/9789264300040-en

ISBN 978-92-64-30003-3 (print)
ISBN 978-92-64-30004-0 (PDF)

The statistical data for Israel are supplied by and under the responsibility of the relevant Israeli authorities. The use of such data by the OECD is without prejudice to the status of the Golan Heights, East Jerusalem and Israeli settlements in the West Bank under the terms of international law.

Photo credits: Cover © gorillaimages/Shutterstock.com.

Preface

Gender equality is both a fundamental human right and a key driver of inclusive growth. Over the past five years, OECD countries have made some progress in getting closer to gender equality goals. The 2013 OECD Recommendation of the Council on Gender Equality in Education, Employment and Entrepreneurship followed in 2015 by the OECD Recommendation of the Council on Gender Equality in Public Life have provided clear and actionable guidelines to support these efforts. However, gender gaps persist in all areas of social and economic life, as the 2017 OECD report *The Pursuit of Gender Equality: An Uphill Battle*, showed.

The Nordic countries – Denmark, Finland, Iceland, Norway and Sweden – have moved further along the path to gender equality than most OECD countries. This report provides ample evidence that increases in women's economic participation in the Nordic countries have greatly benefited economic growth. Indeed, in Denmark, Iceland, Norway and Sweden, increases in women's employment alone accounted for the equivalent of about 10-20% of average annual GDP per capita growth over the past 40-50 years.

The striking feature of the Nordic countries is that they managed to increase and/or sustain female employment rates that were already high even as early as the early-1970s. The long-standing commitment to gender equality at work in Nordic countries has yielded results. Today, gender employment gaps in the Nordic countries are among the OECD's lowest and couples tend to share paid and unpaid work more equally than in most other OECD countries.

The design of gender and work-life balance policies in individual Nordic countries may vary, but they are united by a common policy objective to engage men and women equally in the labour market. With the launch of their initiative Nordic Solutions to Global Challenges in 2017, the five Nordic Prime Ministers expressed their commitment to close gender gaps at home and to share the region's experiences in investing in gender equality and generous work-life policies, which contributed to the development of this report.

Nordic countries are closer to eliminating gender labour market gaps than most, but closing completely the stubborn gaps that remain in areas such as pay and representation in management positions may well turn out to be a difficult challenge. Completing "the last mile" on the path to gender equality would not only bring further economic and social gains to the Nordic countries but also provide important lessons for policy development across the OECD and beyond.

Angel Gurría,
Secretary-General of the OECD

Dagfinn Høybråten
Secretary-General of the Nordic Council of Ministers

Acknowledgements

The report was prepared under the overall supervision of the OECD Secretary-General, Angel Gurría, and the OECD Chief of Staff and Sherpa to the G20, Gabriela Ramos.

The OECD Directorate for Employment, Labour, and Social Affairs (ELS) prepared this report under the senior leadership of Stefano Scarpetta (Director of ELS), Mark Pearson (Deputy Director of ELS) and Monika Queisser (Senior Counsellor, Head of the OECD Social Policy Division and leader of the OECD Horizontal Project on Gender Equality).

The report was written by Willem Adema and Chris Clarke (OECD Social Policy Division). Ulf Andreasson, Truls Stende and Line Christmas Moeller (Nordic Council of Ministers) and Valerie Frey, Mark Keese and Olivier Thévenon (OECD Directorate for Employment, Labour, and Social Affairs) commented on earlier drafts and contributed throughout the preparation process. Liv Gudmundson prepared the report for publication, with Lucy Hulett and Alastair Wood providing further logistical, publication and communications support.

The financial support provided by the Nordic Council of Ministers for this report is gratefully acknowledged.

Table of contents

Tables

Figures

Boxes

Follow OECD Publications on:
http://twitter.com/OECD_Pubs
http://www.facebook.com/OECDPublications
http://www.linkedin.com/groups/OECD-Publications-4645871
http://www.youtube.com/oecdilibrary
OECD
Alerts
http://www.oecd.org/oecddirect/

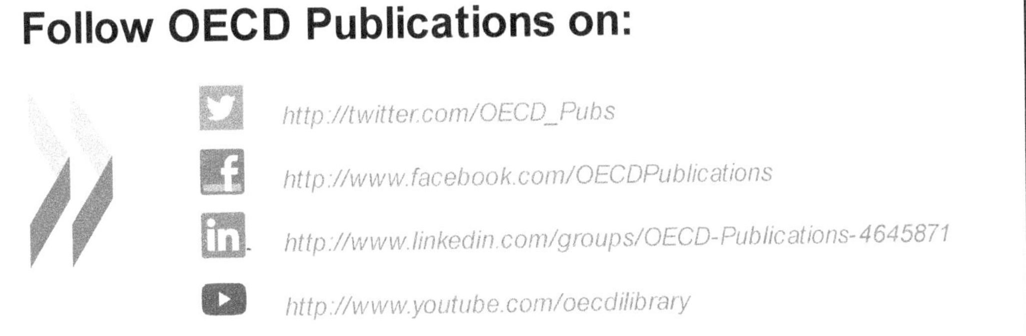

Abbreviations and acronyms

AMECO	Annual macroeconomic database of the European Commission
ECEC	Early childhood education and care
EIGE	European Institute for Gender Equality
EUR	Euro
GDP	Gross domestic product
ICT	Information and communication technology
ILO	International Labour Organization
ISCED	International Standard Classification of Education
ISCO	International Standard Classification of Occupations
LFP	Labour force participation
NEET	Not in employment, education or training
NIKK	Nordic Information on Gender
NOSOSCO	The Nordic Social Statistical Committee
OSH	Out-of-school-hours care
PISA	Programme for International Student Assessment
PPP	Purchasing power parity
PLC	Public limited company
SOE	State-owned enterprise
STEM	Science, technology, engineering and mathematics
USD	United States dollar

Executive summary

Denmark, Finland, Iceland, Norway and Sweden actively promote gender equality at home, at work, and in public life. Promoting gender equality is embedded in the overall Nordic social policy model, including in the provision of universal health, social protection, education and labour market supports, and mainstreamed across the full range of public policies. The policy model also involves a large public sector and tripartite cooperation between employers' organisations, trade unions and the state with collective agreements covering a majority of workers.

The Nordic policy approach aims to encourage all men and women to participate fully in paid employment. Mindful that gender gaps often emerge in full around the time of parenthood, Nordic policy aims to provide a continuum of support to families with children so that both fathers and mothers can pursue their labour market aspirations in full. Parents can access generous paid leave when children are very young, followed by a place in subsidised early childhood education and care (ECEC) and out-of-school-hours (OSH) care activities once children enter full-time education. Furthermore, to encourage fathers to engage more in care work at home, all of the Nordic countries provide paid leave that can only be used by fathers for two to three months, except Denmark which provides two weeks of paid paternity leave.

The Nordic countries have moved further along the path to gender equality than most other OECD countries; since the late 1960s, female employment rates have increased by about 20-25 percentage points, except in Finland where rates were already high. Some other OECD countries, such as France, the United Kingdom and the United States, have seen similar or sometimes even greater increases, but most of them started from a lower base. The striking feature of the Nordic countries is that they managed to increase and sustain female employment rates that were already high in the early 1970s and in 2016 ranged from 67.6% in Finland to 83.4% in Iceland, well above the OECD average of 59.4%.

As a result, labour market outcomes in the Nordic countries are among the most gender-equal in the OECD. Gender gaps in labour force participation and employment are among the OECD's lowest at about 4 percentage points – the OECD average is 12 percentage points. Mothers are more likely to be in (full-time) employment than elsewhere, and couples tend to share paid and unpaid work more equally than in most other OECD countries. However, gender inequalities persist. For example, many women still find it too hard to progress to management positions and gender pay gaps range from 6% in Denmark to 18% in Finland for full-time employees at the median. The OECD average is 14%.

This report shows that, over the past decades, economic growth in the Nordic countries has benefited greatly from increases in women's participation in the labour market. In Denmark, Iceland, Norway and Sweden, increases in female employment account for around 0.25-0.40 percentage points of average annual GDP per capita growth over the past 40-50 years – equivalent to 10-20% of the total GDP per capita growth rate – and a slightly smaller amount in Finland (0.05 percentage points, or about 3%). Converting to cash-equivalent amounts, this implies current GDP per capita in the Nordic countries might have been between USD 1 500 2010 PPP (Finland) and USD 9 000 (Norway) smaller had female employment remained at levels seen in the mid-1960s or early-1970s.

Changes in women's working hours account for a much smaller portion of recent growth, though data availability puts limits on the period over which gains can be assessed. Women's working hours have made the largest estimated contributions to the annual GDP per capita growth rate in Iceland and Norway, at roughly 0.15 percentage points annually, or the equivalent of about 8-9% of total annual GDP per capita growth. Changes in women's working hours had a much smaller effect on growth in Denmark and Sweden while in Finland the decline in women's average working hours had a small negative effect on growth.

Because gender participation gaps are currently small, further narrowing and eventually closing these gaps will have only a limited effect on projected growth in the Nordic countries. For example, closing remaining gender participation gaps by half by 2040 could increase projected annual GDP per capita growth rates by only up to 0.07 percentage points across the Nordic countries.

However, the Nordic countries could make larger gains if they were to narrow or close gender gaps in working hours, as well. Halving existing gender gaps in both participation and hours could add roughly 0.10-0.15 percentage points to projected average annual GDP per capita growth over the years to 2040, while going further and closing both gaps fully could add as much as around 0.25-0.40 percentage points. This would be equivalent to boosting annual GDP per capita growth by roughly 15-30%, depending on the country.

Despite significant progress in some dimensions, gender gaps persist and thus there should be no complacency going forward. Indeed, the Nordic countries are closer than most countries to achieving gender equality in the labour market. But the last mile may well prove to be the longest one.

For example, even in Iceland and Sweden – where fathers are more likely to take parental leave than anywhere else in the OECD – fathers still use less than 30% of all paid leave days, and mothers continue to be the main users of sharable leave. Might policy move towards fully-individualised paid parental leave systems to generate an even better sharing of paid and unpaid work?

It will also take time to address gender stereotypes at large and, for instance, deconstruct gender norms that discourage girls and young women from pursuing a career in the fields of science, technology, engineering or mathematics. To make further progress, a continued assessment of the effectiveness of existing policies and pay transparency initiatives is needed, such as the recently introduced mandatory pay certification in Iceland, to see how workplace practices can be improved. Only with resolve and a continued focus can Nordic countries ensure that men and women have equal labour market opportunities and career prospects and contribute to their economies and societies in gender equal measure.

1. Overview

The Nordic countries have long been international champions of gender equality. Denmark, Finland, Iceland, Norway and Sweden – commonly known as the Nordic countries[*] – explicitly support gender equality at home, at work, and in public life, and have often moved earlier and faster than most countries in taking action to promote this goal. They were among the first countries in the world to provide women with full voting rights, for example, and some of the earliest to introduce legislation prohibiting dismissal from employment on the grounds of marriage or parenthood (Hilson, 2007[1]; Statistics Sweden, 2016[2]). Over the past 50 years, the Nordic countries have been leaders in the development of modern family and gender equality policy, which promotes gender equality in the labour market. They were some of the earliest to establish comprehensive public early childhood education and care (ECEC) services, for instance, and the very first to introduce the so-called "mother and father quotas" as part of paid parental leave systems (*OECD Family Database;* Section 2).

The Nordic countries have yet to achieve full gender equality in the labour market, but they have travelled further along the path than most OECD countries. Gender gaps in labour participation and employment are among the OECD's lowest, particularly among highly-educated men and women (Table 1.1). Mothers are more likely to be in work than elsewhere (*OECD Family Database*), gender differences in working hours are comparatively small (Table 1.1), and couples tend to share paid work more equally than in most other OECD countries (OECD, 2017[3]). However, some large gender gaps persist. For example, foreign-born women are under-represented in paid work (OECD, 2016[4]), occupational sex-segregation may be falling but is still high (Ellingsæter, 2013[5]; Teigen and Skjeie, 2017[6]), and many women still find it too hard to progress to management positions (Table 1.1). Gender pay gaps vary – from roughly 6% in Denmark to 18% in Finland for full-time employees – but persist (Table 1.1).

Promoting gender equality is likely to carry a number of benefits for societies and economies. Providing girls and women with equal opportunities is an issue of human rights and holds intrinsic value in and of itself, but there are also social and economic effects that mean wider society is better off when women are treated fairly. Societies that are more gender-equal tend also to be happier (Looze et al., 2017[7]), healthier (Van de Velde et al., 2013[8]; Holter, 2014[9]), and more trusting (Cho, 2016[10]), for example. They are often also more equal and inclusive. Previous work by the OECD, for instance, has shown that having more women in work can help reduce income inequality, especially when it involves full-time work by low-skilled women (OECD, 2015[11]).

---

[*]The Åland Islands, the Faroe Islands and Greenland are not included in this study for practical reasons as it is not possible to extract statistics in the same way as for Denmark, Finland, Iceland Norway and Sweden.

Table 1.1. The Nordic countries boast some of the most gender-equal labour markets in the OECD, but there is still more to do

Key measures of gender gaps in employment, Nordic and selected other OECD countries, 2016 or latest available year

	Top performer	Moderate performer	Bottom performer				
	Gender gap in the labour force participation rate, 15-64 year-olds (p.p.)	Gender gap in the employment rate, 15-64 year-olds (p.p.)	Gender gap in the employment rate, low education, 25-64 year-olds (p.p.)	Gender gap in the employment rate, high education, 25-64 year-olds (p.p.)	Gender gap in usual weekly working hours, all ages (p.p.)	Female share of managers, all ages (%)	Gender gap in median earnings for full-time employees, all ages (%)
Denmark	6.3	6.2	17.9	4.9	4.2	27.3	5.8
Finland	3.0	2.0	16.7	4.0	4.0	33.8	18.1
Iceland	4.8	4.8	11.3	5.5	8.4	33.3	9.9
Norway	4.3	3.6	11.3	1.4	4.8	37.8	7.1
Sweden	3.6	3.0	13.7	1.5	3.6	39.4	13.4
Canada	7.6	6.1	19.7	6.7	5.6	35.5	18.2
France	7.9	6.4	13.9	5.8	5.6	32.9	9.9
Germany	9.1	8.0	16.4	6.7	8.7	29.3	15.5
Italy	20.0	18.3	30.8	10.0	7.3	27.7	5.6
Japan	18.2	17.2	..	21.1	..	13.0	25.7
United Kingdom	10.3	9.4	20.6	8.0	9.0	36.0	16.8
United States	11.5	10.8	25.2	9.8	4.0	43.4	18.1
OECD average	12.2	11.4	20.4	8.7	5.9	32.3	14.1
OECD std. dev.	8.0	7.8	9.0	5.5	2.5	8.0	7.2

Reading note: Shading indicates performance relative to the OECD average and the OECD standard deviation. For measures where a smaller value is generally "better" (e.g. "Gender gap in the labour force participation rate"), "top performer" means a value less than the OECD average by more than half the OECD standard deviation (s.d.), and "bottom performer" a value greater than the OECD average by more than half an s.d. For measures where a larger value is better (e.g. "Female share of managers"), "top performer" means a value greater than the OECD average by more than half an s.d., and "bottom performer" a value less than the OECD average by more than half an s.d. In both cases "moderate performer" means a value within half an s.d. of the OECD average, either way.

Notes: The OECD average and OECD standard deviation are unweighted and refer to the average/standard deviation across all OECD members with available data. Low educational attainment is defined as a highest level of educational attainment at ISCED 2011 levels 0-2, and high educational attainment as a highest level of educational attainment at ISCED 2011 levels 5-8. Average usual weekly working hours refer to usual hours in the main job, only. Data refer to all employed, except for the United States where they refer to dependent employees only. Data on managers refer to those employed in ISCO-08 category one (as managers), or for Canada, Chile, and the United States, in ISCO-88 category one (as legislators, senior officials and managers). Data for the United States refer to 2013 and for Canada to 2014. The gender gap in median earnings is defined as men's median earnings minus women's median earnings, divided by men's median earnings. Data for Sweden refer to 2013, for Italy and France to 2014, and for Denmark, Finland, Iceland, Japan, and Norway to 2015.

Source: OECD Employment Database (http://www.oecd.org/employment/emp/onlineoecdemploymentdatabase.htm); OECD (2017), *OECD Education at a Glance 2017: OECD Indicators*, OECD Publishing, Paris (http://www.oecd.org/education/education-at-a-glance-19991487.htm); ILO ILOSTAT Database (http://www.ilo.org/ilostat); and Statistics Canada (https://www.statcan.gc.ca/eng/start).

There are also strong economic reasons to strive for gender equality. More gender-equal economies tend to be more prosperous economies (Goldin, 1995[12]; Klasen, 1999[13]; Klasen and Lamanna, 2009[14]), for various reasons. Promoting women's employment and hours can help boost labour supply (Østbakken, 2016[15]), for example, while making better use of the increasingly-well-educated female talent pool and improving job match can help deliver productivity gains (Esteve-Volart, 2004[16]; Hsieh et al., 2013[17]; Cuberes and Teignier, 2015[18]). Indeed, OECD (2012[19])found that gains in educational attainment can account for roughly half of all economic growth in OECD countries over the 1960-2007 period – much of which can be traced back to increased educational attainment among girls and young women and the associated benefits for employment and productivity. Put simply, gender equality is good not only for women, but also for men and for families, for growth, and for society as a whole.

Increasingly, policy-makers around the world are recognising the economic gains that can be made from promoting gender equality. For example, at their November 2014 Summit in Brisbane, the leaders of the G20 countries committed to reducing the gender gap in labour force participation by 25% by 2025 (OECD et al., 2014[20]). Achieving this goal would bring millions more women into the workforce worldwide, and significantly increase growth across the OECD and the G20 (OECD, 2017[21]).

This report explores the extent to which past improvements in gender equality in the labour market have contributed to economic growth in Nordic countries (and G7 countries for comparison), and how much more could be gained from closing gender gaps still further. For data reasons, it concentrates on the quantitative aspects of labour market equality – how much do women work, and how does this compare to men? – leaving aspects like potential productivity gains aside.

The analysis shows that the Nordic countries have benefited hugely from the progress in women's employment in recent decades, but that there is still more to be gained. Potential benefits from narrowing and ultimately closing gender gaps in labour participation and in working hours are smaller in the Nordic countries than elsewhere, largely because the remaining gaps themselves are comparatively small. Alas, the last mile may well prove to be the longest one. Completing it would bring economic and social gains to the Nordic countries and also provide important lessons for policy development across the OECD and beyond.

1.1. The Nordic approach to family- and gender-equality policy

All OECD countries provide family and gender-equality policies in at least some form, though the types and intensity of support often differ. Differences in countries' histories, labour markets, attitudes towards families and gender norms, the role of government, and the relative weight given to the various underlying policy objectives all mean that each country takes its own approach to family and gender policy (see, for example, Thévenon (2011[22]) and Adema (2012[23]) for a discussion and overview).

The Nordic approach to family and gender-equality policy grew largely out of the principles of 'work friendliness' and full participation embedded at the centre of the wider Nordic welfare state (Kuhnle and Hort, 2004[24]; Brandth et al., 2012[25]; Pedersen and Kuhnle, 2017[26]). The model is geared towards facilitating employment for all adults where possible, with the state expected to provide them with the services and supports necessarily to do so – including family supports like childcare and paid leave needed to help men and women find and stay in paid employment (Esping-Andersen, 1999[27]; Kuhnle and Hort, 2004[24]).

Today, the Nordic countries provide some of the most comprehensive packages of family and gender-equality policy in the OECD in line with the principles of the OECD Gender

Recommendations (OECD, 2017[28]; OECD, 2016[29]). The specifics vary from country to country, but the general emphasis is on encouraging continuous full-time employment for all men and women, including single parents, and promoting a "dual earner-dual carer" family model (Section 2.4). Recognising that gender gaps often emerge in full around the time of parenthood, policy looks to provide families with children with a 'continuum' of supports allowing parents to stay in paid work as children grow up. Parents can access generous paid leave when children are very young, followed by a place in subsidised early childhood education and care (ECEC) and out-of-school-hours (OSH) care activities once children enter full-time education. Tax and benefit systems are also largely individualised (Pedersen and Kuhnle, 2017[26]), so as not to discourage paid work by second earners, and fathers and mothers are encouraged to share care responsibilities by means of individualised "use it or lose it" paid leave entitlements (Section 2.4.2).

However, there are some important policy differences across the Nordic countries. For example, both Finland and Norway provide "home care" or "cash-for-care" allowances to parents with very young children when at least one parent stays home (*OECD Family Database*). Even though actual payment rates may not seem high, they can discourage second-earners from engaging in paid work, at least in the first few years after childbirth (Section 2.4.2). These variations do matter, and may help explain some of the small but important differences in outcomes between Nordic countries. The Finnish home care allowance, for instance, helps to explain why Finnish mothers with very young children are less likely to be found in paid work than mothers in the other Nordic countries (OECD, 2005[30]; OECD, 2016[31]).

1.2. The Nordic model has helped deliver large gains in gender equality in employment over the past half-century

The Nordic policy approach has helped deliver and sustain large improvements in gender labour market equality over recent decades. The scale of some of the gains made in the Nordic countries, especially on female employment rates, is remarkable. In Sweden, for example, the working-age (15-64) female employment rate increased by almost 30 percentage points (from 52.8% to 81.0%) over the 25 years between 1965 and 1990 (*OECD Employment Database*) – equivalent to jumping from a level that would today be one of the OECD's lowest to its second highest in just 25 years. Female employment has fallen slightly since, especially following the economic crisis in the early-1990s (see below), but remains more than 20 percentage points higher than it was in the mid-1960s (Figure 1.1, Panel A). Denmark, Iceland and Norway have made similar gains since the mid-1960s or early-1970s, while Finland, which already had a high female employment rate in 1970, has made much smaller gains (Figure 1.1, Panel A).

What is particularly impressive about these gains is that they occurred on top of initial rates that were already comparatively high. Some other OECD countries have also seen female employment increase by the same or sometimes even greater amounts over similar periods, but for the most part they started from a lower base (Figure 1.1, Panel A). For example, France, the United Kingdom and the United States have all seen the working-age female employment rate increase by between 15 and 25 percentage points since the early-1960s or 1970s, but all started the period on rates of roughly 45% (Figure 1.1, Panel A). Denmark, Iceland and Sweden, by contrast, built their gains on female employment rates that were already around 55% – rates that are higher than several OECD countries, including Chile, Italy and Mexico, even today (*OECD Employment Database*).

Figure 1.1. The Nordic countries have made large gains on female employment in recent decades, even from an already high base, and these gains have boosted economic growth

Panel A. Female employment rate, 15-64 year-olds, earliest available year and latest available year (2016), Nordic and selected other OECD member countries

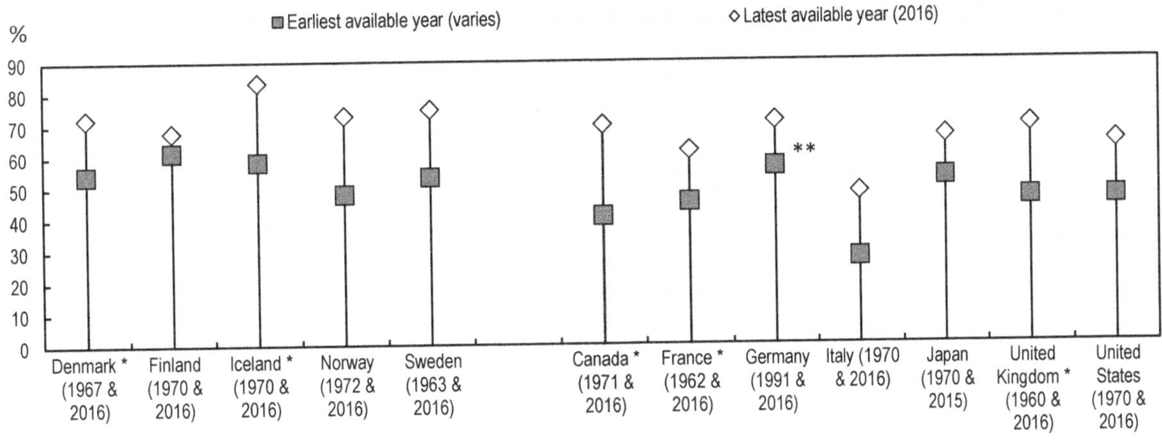

Panel B. Average annual rate of growth in GDP per capita and disaggregation of growth into its primary components, longest available series, Nordic and selected other OECD member countries

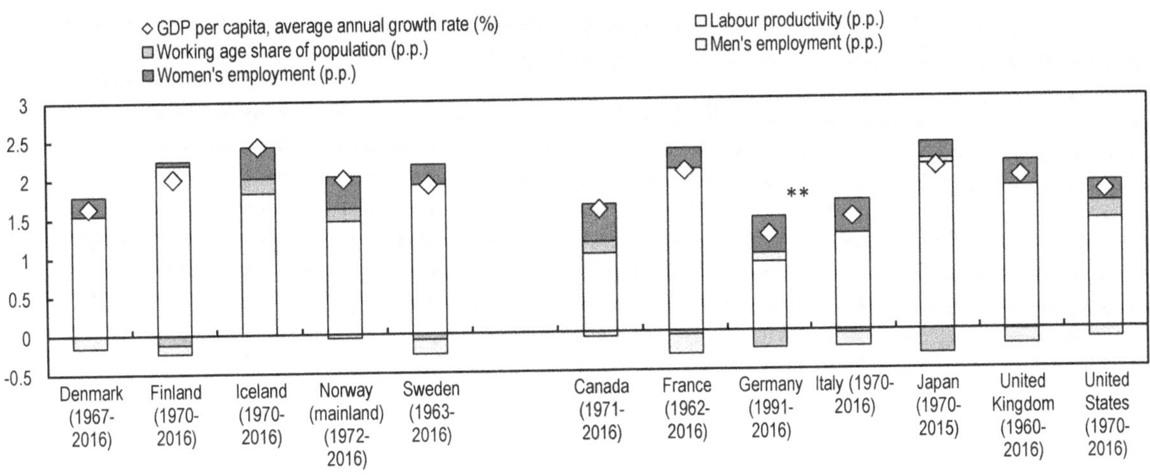

Note for Panel A: For countries marked with an *, data for the earliest available year are estimated. See Annex B for more detail. For Germany, the earliest year (1991) is much later than for the other countries so should not be compared directly.

Note for Panel B: Estimates based on the decomposition of national accounts data using labour force survey estimates. Differences in the time periods covered mean estimates are not fully comparable across countries, especially for Germany (1991). See Section 3 and Annex B for more detail.

Sources: Panel A: *OECD Employment Database* (http://www.oecd.org/employment/emp/onlineoecdemploymentdatabase.htm), and OECD estimates based on data from the *OECD Annual Labour Force Statistics Database* (http://stats.oecd.org/index.aspx?queryid=451), Eurostat (http://ec.europa.eu/eurostat/data/database), and national statistical offices (see Annex B); Panel B: OECD estimates based on data from the *OECD National Accounts Database* (http://www.oecd.org/std/na/), the *OECD Employment Database* (http://www.oecd.org/employment/emp/onlineoecdemploymentdatabase.htm), the European Commission's *AMECO Database* (http://ec.europa.eu/economy_finance/ameco/user/serie/SelectSerie.cfm), Eurostat (http://ec.europa.eu/eurostat/data/database), and national statistical offices (see Annex B).

Employment patterns in the Nordic countries do not escape fluctuations with the economic cycle. Across the Nordic countries, women's employment has tended to hold up better than men's employment in the immediate aftermath of shocks like the economic crisis in the early-1990s (Finland and Sweden) or the Great Recession (e.g. Iceland), leading to reduced gender employment gaps (Table A A.1 in Annex A). However, in most cases men's employment also recovered quicker, so that five to ten years later, gender employment gaps had returned to levels similar to before the relevant crisis (Table A A.1 in Annex A). Gender working hours gaps in the Nordic countries seem to be affected less than employment gaps by economic fluctuations, in most cases holding steady through recessions and recoveries. The exception is Iceland, where men's working hours fell sharply following the Great Recession, leading to a three-hour (or 23%) reduction in the gender gap in weekly working just in the years three between 2007 and 2010 (Table A A.2 in Annex A).

1.3. Gains in women's employment can account for a large portion of economic growth in the Nordic countries

Gains in gender equality, and especially gains in female headcount employment, have made a substantial contribution to economic growth in the Nordic countries over the past 50 years or so. Growth accounting estimates suggest that, in Denmark, Iceland, Norway and Sweden, increases in women's employment account for around 0.25-0.40 percentage points of the annual GDP per capita growth rate since the mid-1960s or early-1970s – roughly equivalent to 10-20% of the overall average annual growth rate. The contribution in Finland is smaller, at 0.05 percentage points on average over the years since 1970 (Figure 1.1, Panel B).

As always with this kind of exercise, these estimates should be interpreted with a certain degree of caution – in this instance, it is important to recognise they are based on a mechanical decomposition of the drivers of growth only, and do not account for any gender differences in productivity (see Section 3 and Annex B for details). Nonetheless, these estimates are large. Converting to equivalent cash amounts,[1] current GDP per capita in Denmark and Sweden would be around USD 5 000-6 000 (2010 PPP) smaller if the parts of growth accounted for by increases in women's employment were removed from the historic growth rate. In Iceland, current GDP per capita would be roughly USD 7 500 smaller, while in Norway (mainland) it would be close to USD 9 000 smaller. Even in Finland, current GDP per capita would be about USD 1 500 smaller if the (comparatively small) contribution from changes in women's employment was removed from historic growth. These are significant numbers. Losing these amounts would be equivalent to seeing GDP per capita return to levels last seen in the late-1990s or early-2000s across all five of the Nordic countries.

There is less evidence of large contributions from changes in women's working hours. Gender differences in working hours have actually fallen slightly in the Nordic countries in recent decades, but this is due more to a decline in men's hours (a common trend in most OECD countries) than any real increase in women's average working hours. Changes in women's hours in paid work account for only a fairly small portion of average annual GDP per capita growth in the Nordic countries, at least in comparison to women's headcount employment. Of the five Nordic counties, women's hours have made the largest contributions in Iceland and Norway, where they account for the equivalent of roughly 8-9% of the overall average annual GDP per capita growth rate. Contributions from changes in women's hours are much smaller in Denmark and Sweden, and even slightly negative in Finland, where female average weekly working hours have declined by just over two hours per week since 1990.

The muted trends in female average working hours in recent decades contribute to the relatively small effects on GDP growth. It is quite possible that changes in working hours in the 1960s and 1970s (when the development of ECEC systems may have contributed to a move from part-time to full-time employment for many women) were more pronounced. Unfortunately, data on average working hours disaggregated by gender are comparatively scarce, and the time period covered by these working hours estimates (for the most part, the mid-to-late-1980s onwards) is generally much shorter than the period for headcount employment (the mid-1960s or 1970s onwards).

1.4. Further gains from closing gender participation gaps are limited, but potential gains from closing gender working hours gaps are larger

Because the current gender participation gaps in Nordic countries are relatively small, closing these gaps is likely to have a fairly limited impact on future GDP per capita growth. OECD projections suggest that, for the Nordic countries, even fully closing the remaining gender participation gaps by the year 2040 would boost projected average annual GDP per capita growth over the period to 2040 by only roughly 0.05-0.10 percentage points, with the largest potential gains in Denmark (Figure 1.2). This is a fairly small potential gain compared to the historic gains related to increases in female employment over the past half-century, and pale in comparison to the potential gains still on offer in countries with larger participation gaps such as Italy.

However, the Nordics could still make large gains from closing remaining gender *working hours* gaps. These gaps, while small in comparison to some other OECD countries, are still considerable and offer much more scope for progress. Across all five Nordic countries, fully closing gender gaps in both labour participation rates *and* average weekly working hours through increases by women could add as much as around 0.25-0.40 percentage points to the average annual rate of GDP per capita growth over the period to 2040 (Figure 1.2) – the equivalent of boosting the projected annual GDP per capita growth rate by roughly 15-30%, depending on the country. The largest potential future gains (ranging from 0.35 to 0.42 percentage points) can be made in Denmark and Norway, where women's current average working hours are relatively low at around 30-32 hours per week hours per week (Figure 3.4), and in Iceland, where men's working hours are relatively high at over 43 hours per week (Figure A A.2. in Annex A). In terms of overall growth over the 2013-2040 period, these potential gains are equivalent to boosting cumulative GDP per capita growth by somewhere between 12 (Finland and Sweden) and 19 percentage points (Denmark). In dollar terms, they would translate by 2040 into increases in GDP per capita (relative to the baseline) of around USD 3 900 (2005 PPP) in Finland, USD 4 300 in Sweden, USD 5 600 in Iceland, USD 6 100 in Denmark and USD 8 200 in Norway.

Figure 1.2. Fully closing remaining gender gaps in both participation and working hours could provide a sizeable boost to economic growth

Estimated gains relative to the baseline in the projected average annual rate of growth in GDP per capita over the period 2013-2040, different gender gap scenarios (closing gender gaps in labour force participation and working hours), percentage points, Nordic and selected other OECD member countries

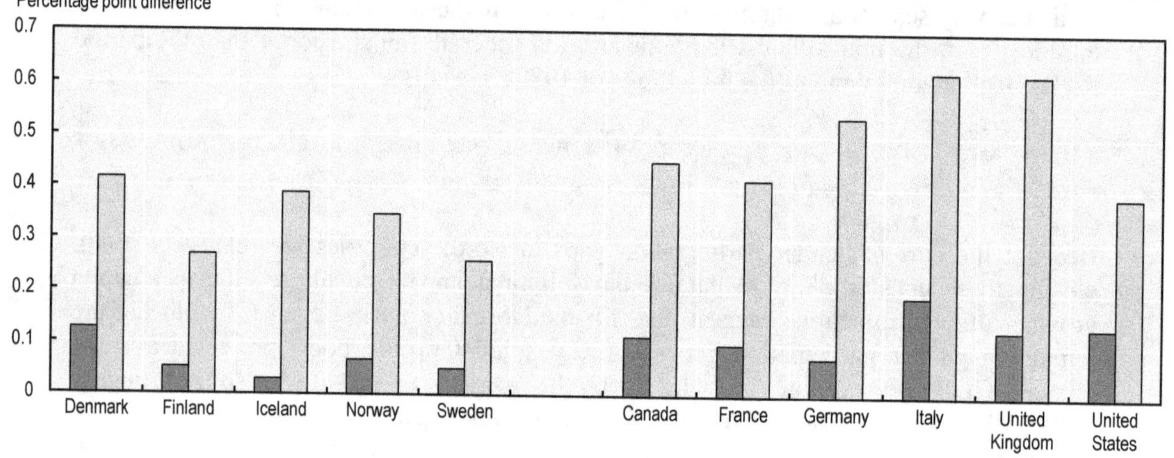

Note: See Section 4 and Annex B for more details.
Source: OECD estimates based on OECD (2014), *OECD Economic Outlook No. 95 Volume 2014 Issue 1*, OECD Publishing, Paris (http://dx.doi.org/10.1787/eco_outlook-v2014-1-en), *OECD Economic Outlook: Statistics and Projections Databases* (http://stats.oecd.org/index.aspx?dataSetCode=EO), OECD population data and the *OECD Employment Database* (http://www.oecd.org/employment/emp/onlineoecdemploymentdatabase.htm).

Whether or not it is feasible or even desirable to fully close gender gaps in this manner is a matter for debate. In recent years, much of the discussion in the Nordic countries has centred on the possibility of further *reducing* working hours to promote well-being – see the 2016/17 six-hour workday experiments in Sweden, for instance – but closing gaps just by raising women's participation and hours would actually involve a considerable *increase* in overall hours worked. In Iceland, for example, it would mean both men *and* women working an average of roughly 43 hours per week. This would limit time available for unpaid work and put strain on families' abilities to juggle work and care. Closing gender gaps in a more gender-balanced way – say, with men reducing their working hours to some extent, in addition to increases from women – might provide a more realistic middle-ground (though likely with smaller economic gains). Nonetheless, the scenarios summarised above provide at least an illustration of the potential room or scope for further economic gains from closing gender gaps in the Nordic countries.

2. Gender equality in the Nordic countries: Good progress, but more to do

The Nordic countries do well on gender equality, but there is more to do. This section provides an overview of the state of gender equality and gender equality policy in the Nordic countries, comparing these with each other and with other OECD countries. It starts with gender outcomes in education (Section 2.1) as educational performance precedes labour market participation, and indeed is a key driver of labour market outcomes of men and women (Section 2.2). Section 2.3 looks at the Nordic approach to welfare policy in general, and Section 2.4 at gender equality and family policy in particular.

2.1. Boys underperforming at school is a key education concern, but girls are under-represented in STEM subjects

Getting a good education is a central determinant of life-chances in OECD countries, and providing boys and girls with equal opportunities at school is key to ensuring equal labour market opportunities. The Nordic countries, like all OECD countries, have made huge progress on closing gender differences in education in recent decades. Five or six decades ago, girls and young women were far less likely than boys and young men to attain secondary education and especially a university degree (Barro and Lee, 2013[32]), but today, on average, they obtain higher levels of educational attainment than their male peers (see e.g. Barro and Lee (2013[32]) and the *OECD Education Database*).

More so than in other OECD countries, education concerns in the Nordic countries currently relate more to the underperformance of boys in school than to the performance of girls (OECD, 2016[33]; OECD, 2016[34]; OECD, 2018[35]). At age 15, girls on average outperform boys in OECD's PISA (Programme for International Student Assessment) reading tests in all OECD countries, but nowhere more so than in the Nordic countries (Table 2.1). Furthermore, Finland is the only OECD country where girls significantly outperform boys on the PISA maths test, and Denmark the only Nordic country where boys outperform girls. In the other three Nordic countries (Iceland, Norway and Sweden), girls do just as well as boys on mathematics. These performance gaps at age 15 contribute to large gender gaps in the numbers that go on to receive a university education: in 2015, young women (aged 25-34) in the Nordic countries were around 14-18 percentage points more likely than young men to complete tertiary education (Table 2.1).

Table 2.1. On gender, the Nordic countries compare favourably to other OECD countries

Key indicators of gender gaps in education, employment and entrepreneurship, Nordic and selected other OECD countries, 2016 or latest available year

	Education			Employment			Entrepre-neurship
	Gender gap in mean PISA reading scores, 15 year-olds (score points)	Gender gap in mean PISA mathematics scores, 15 year-olds (score points)	Gender gap in the share that have attained tertiary education, 25-34 year-olds (p.p.)	Gender gap in the labour force participation rate, 15-64 year-olds (p.p.)	Female share of part-time employment, all ages (%)	Gender gap in median earnings for full-time employees, all ages (%)	Gender gap in the share of employed who are employers, 15-64 year-olds (p.p.)
Denmark	-22.2 *	9.4 *	-14.3	6.3	57.7	5.8	2.9
Finland	-46.5 *	-7.5 *	-16.3	3.0	60.8	18.1	3.9
Iceland	-41.6 *	-1.1	-17.5	4.8	65.1	9.9	3.3
Norway	-39.8 *	-2.3	-17.0	4.3	67.1	7.1	1.7
Sweden	-39.2 *	-2.2	-15.9	3.6	61.8	13.4	3.6
Canada	-26.2 *	9.0 *	-18.2	7.6	65.6	18.2	3.3
France	-29.1 *	6.0	-9.3	7.9	74.7	9.9	3.7
Germany	-20.8 *	16.6 *	-1.9	9.1	78.1	15.5	3.5
Italy	-16.0 *	19.9 *	-12.2	20.0	73.6	5.6	3.9
Japan	-13.3 *	13.8 *	-4.0	18.2	70.3	25.7	2.1
United Kingdom	-21.9 *	11.6 *	-2.8	10.3	74.1	16.8	1.8
United States	-20.1 *	8.5 *	-8.1	11.5	65.8	18.1	2.1
OECD average	-26.9 *	7.9 *	-11.5	12.2	68.1	14.1	3.3
OECD std. dev.	9.6	7.4	6.5	8.0	6.5	7.2	0.8

Legend: Top performer / Moderate performer / Bottom performer

Reading note: Shading indicates performance relative to the OECD average and the OECD standard deviation. "Top performer" means a value less than the OECD average by more than half the OECD standard deviation (s.d.), and "bottom performer" a value greater than the OECD average by more than half an s.d. "Moderate performer" means a value within half an s.d. of the OECD average, either way. For the indicators of gender gaps in education, "top performer" indicates a gender gap more strongly in favour of girls/young women, and "bottom performer" a gender gap more strongly in favour of boys/young men.

Note: Data on PISA scores refer to 2015. Where marked with an *, the gender gap in the mean PISA score on the given test subject is statistically significant. "Tertiary education" refers to all types of tertiary-level qualifications (ISCED 2011 Levels 5-8). Part-time employment is defined as average usual weekly working hours in the main job of less than 30 hours per week. Data refer to all employed, except for the United States where they refer to dependent employees only. The gender gap in median earnings is defined as men's median earnings minus women's median earnings, divided by men's median earnings. Data for Sweden refer to 2013, for Italy and France to 2014, and for Denmark, Finland, Iceland, Japan, and Norway to 2015. The "share of the employed who are employers" is the share of the employed that are self-employed and have employees. Data for Canada, the United States, and the OECD average refer to 2015. Data for the United States concern 16-64 year-olds.

Source: OECD PISA 2015 Database (http://www.oecd.org/pisa/data); OECD (2016), *OECD Education at a Glance 2017: OECD Indicators*, OECD Publishing, Paris (http://www.oecd.org/education/education-at-a-glance-19991487.htm); *OECD Employment Database*, (http://www.oecd.org/employment/emp/onlineoecdemploymentdatabase.htm); OECD (2017), *Entrepreneurship at a Glance 2017*, OECD Publishing, Paris (http://www.oecd.org/industry/business-stats/entrepreneurship-at-a-glance-22266941.htm).

However, as elsewhere in the OECD, girls and young women remain much less likely to study science, technology, engineering or mathematics (STEM) subjects. In Denmark, Finland, Norway and Sweden only one-third or less of tertiary graduates in STEM subjects are women (no comparable data are available for Iceland), with this sometimes falling as low as around 15-20% in some sub-fields like information and communication technology (*OECD Education Database*). Almost all OECD countries face a similar problem – the OECD average female share of tertiary graduates in STEM is just 31% – but it seems especially surprising for the Nordic countries given that Nordic girls do so well on the OECD PISA mathematics tests (Table 2.1). Stoet and Geary (2018[36]) suggest that a combination of personal academic strength in reading, lower interest in science, and broader financial security help explain why so few women in highly developed countries choose STEM careers, while women are more likely to choose STEM in countries with fewer economic opportunities.

Gender gaps in education and career aspirations start to form very early in life. Data from the OECD's PISA tests show that even by age 15, boys and girls have already developed very different career expectations (OECD, 2015[37]). OECD-wide, 15-year-old boys are, on average, more than twice as likely as girls to expect to work as engineers, scientists or architects, and ten times more likely to want to be an ICT professional. By contrast, girls are much more likely to expect a career as a health worker or teacher (OECD, 2017[21]). These gender gaps in career expectations are related more to attitudes than aptitudes (OECD, 2015[37]), which only serves to underline the importance of tackling stereotypes and changing views on suitable career paths early on.

Policy-makers in the Nordic countries and in other OECD countries are increasingly introducing measures to address gender stereotyping at school and encourage girls to study STEM subjects (OECD, 2017[28]; OECD, 2017[21]). In Sweden, for instance, the revised 2010 Swedish pre-school curriculum explicitly seeks to counteract traditional gender patterns and gender roles (Skolverket, 2011[38]). To promote a better gender balance in some fields of study the Norwegian government will award from the academic year 2018-2019 onwards extra "study points" to applicants of the under-represented gender for some studies, e.g. men who choose to study nursing and women who choose selected engineering studies (Government of Norway, 2018[39]).

Still, much more can be done, in the Nordic countries as elsewhere. As discussed in more depth in OECD (OECD, 2015[37]) and OECD (2017[21]), training teachers to recognise (and address) any biases they themselves may hold about gender roles (as Sweden has done) could help them teach both girls *and* boys more effectively, while reviewing school curricula and resources (like textbooks) for biases can help prevent the reinforcement of stereotypes within school itself. Career counselling in schools and mentoring programmes can also be introduced from a young age to challenge girls' and boys' perceptions of gender stereotypes and open up awareness of alternative career paths. Despite these initiatives and prevailing gender-equality policies (see below) gender stereotypes persist and future work may consider how best to address gender stereotyping also considering the role the media and social media play in perpetuating existing gender roles.

2.2. Gender labour market gaps are often small but pay gaps are persistent

The relatively high levels of female educational attainment in the Nordic countries contribute to relatively small gender gaps in labour force participation. Except for Denmark, gender labour force participation gaps are less than five percentage points (Table 2.1), far lower than the OECD average (about 12 percentage points). Apart from Switzerland (where many women work part-time), Denmark, Iceland, Norway and Sweden are the only OECD countries with female participation rates exceed 75%, with Finland close behind on 74% (*OECD Employment Database*). Gender gaps in part-time employment and especially average working hours are also relatively small compared to

OECD and G7 countries (around four hours per week, compared to an OECD average of about six hours per week), except in Iceland, where men are in paid work for an average of 43 hours per week, compared to 35 hours per week for women (Table 1.1; Table 2.1; *OECD Employment Database*).

While gender participation gaps are small, women in the Nordic countries are still less likely than men to progress in their careers and remain under-represented in management positions (Figure 2.1). In Denmark, for example, women make up about 27% of managers despite composing 47% of the labour force. The female share of managers higher in Finland (34%) and more so Iceland, Norway and Sweden (38-39%), but the "leaky pipeline" still exists and is more pronounced than in the United States, for example (Figure 2.1).

In 2008, Norway became the first country in the world to introduce a legislated quota for the gender composition of both public limited company (PLC) and state-owned enterprise (SOE) boards, prescribing that at least 40% of board members come from both sexes. Similar legislation came into force in Iceland in 2013 (OECD, 2012[19]), with the other Nordic countries opting for a more voluntary approach. Compared to most OECD countries, the Nordic countries perform relatively well on women's representation on boards. Of the five Nordics, Denmark has the lowest female share of PLC board members (25%) and Iceland the highest (45%) (OECD, 2017[21]). Women's representation is sometimes a little higher in state-owned enterprises – in Sweden, for instance, 49% of chairs and directors in wholly and partially state-owned enterprises are women (Government Offices of Sweden, 2016[40]). Still, more broadly, parity is often some way off and in many ways the glass ceiling is still there to be broken.

Figure 2.1. Nordic countries have not yet plugged the leaky pipeline

Female share of management employment and female share of labour force, all ages, 2016

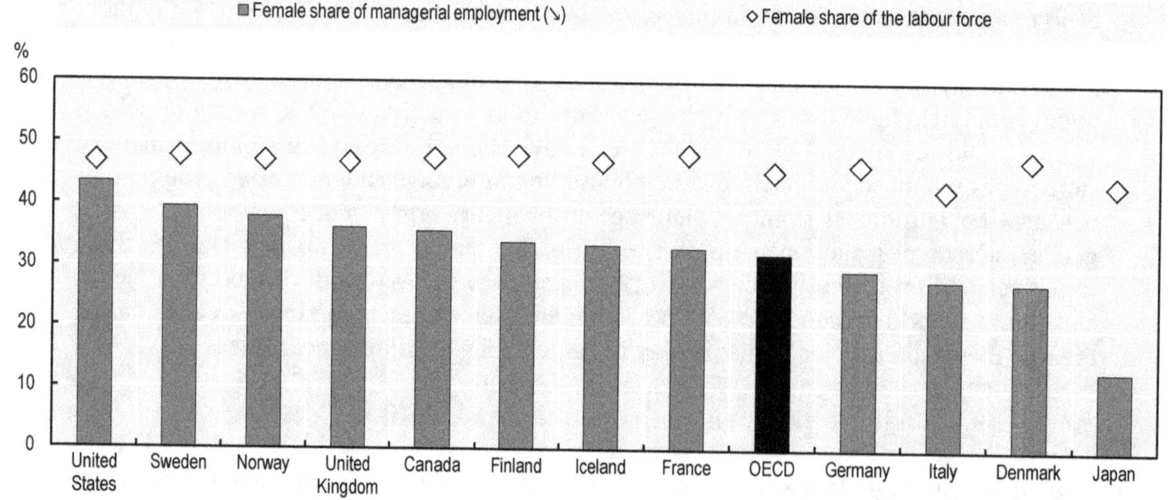

Note: Data on the female share of managers refer to women's share of those employed in ISCO-08 category one (as managers), or for Canada and the United States, in ISCO-88 category one (as legislators, senior officials and managers). Data for Canada refer to 2014 and the United States to 2013.
Source: *OECD Employment Database* (http://www.oecd.org/employment/emp/onlineoecdemploymentdatabase.htm); and OECD calculations based on the *ILO ILOSTAT Database* (http://www.ilo.org/ilostat).

Women in the Nordic countries are less likely to be entrepreneurs than in most other OECD countries (*OECD Gender Data Portal*) and gender gaps in the incidence of entrepreneurship are often close to the OECD average or above (OECD, 2017[21]) (Table 2.1). Policy tries to promote women entrepreneurship, and to this end Sweden, for example has had business development programmes for many years including advisory services and training; the current "national strategy for business promotion on equal terms (women, youth and foreign-born) covers the period 2015-20 (OECD, 2017[41]). Alas, the work-life balance supports that are embodied in the Nordic policy model (see below) give women better employment options than in many other countries and reduce the need to use self-employment as a tool to reconcile work and family commitments (Kelley et al., 2017[42]; OECD, 2012[19]).

Another feature of the family-friendly employment conditions in Nordic countries is that most employees are covered by collective labour agreements which provide employees with some control over their working time arrangements. More than anywhere else in Europe, over 60% of employees in Denmark, Norway and Sweden have at least some control over working hours, which can make it easier to match working hours with opening hours of ECEC-services and schools (OECD, 2016[43]). Similarly, around 40% of employees in Denmark, Finland, Norway, and Sweden work from home, at least occasionally, while this is 20% or less in most other European countries. At 70% or more employees in Denmark, Finland, Ireland, the Netherlands, Norway and Sweden are also among the most likely to be able to take off for one or two hours for personal/family reasons, e.g. take a child to the dentist (OECD, 2016[43]).

The public sector is large in the Nordic countries and, at around 70%, the female share of public employment is well above the OECD average of 60% (OECD, 2017[44]). Women often prefer working in the public sector as family-friendly work place supports are widely available and the penalty for using them is much smaller than in the private sector (Nielsen, Simonsen and Verner, 2004[45]). Nevertheless, also in the public sector, are women still under-represented in management positions: in 2015, the female share of managers in central government ranged from 35% in Finland to 55% in Iceland (OECD, 2017[44]).

In terms of gender pay gaps, the Nordic countries score close to the OECD average (14.3%) when considering median monthly earnings for full-time workers. Available data for Denmark and Iceland are based on hourly earnings, and as a result tend to underestimate the pay gap relative to other countries using monthly earnings (OECD, 2017[21]). In the Nordic countries, as in other OECD countries, gender pay differentials widen once children appear in the household (Angelov and Lindahl, 2016[46]; Gallen, Lesner and Vejlin, 2017[47]; Kleven, Landais and Søgaard, 2018[48]). For example, Swedish data suggest that the relatively low intensity of labour force participation during the five years after the first childbirth can explain most of the female disadvantage in career and pay profiles (Keloharju, Knüpfer and Tåg, 2017[49]).

Gender segregation in the Nordic labour markets has fallen slightly in recent years but remains high (Ellingsæter, 2013[5]; Teigen and Skjeie, 2017[6]). Employed women in particular are disproportionately likely to be found working in the (large) public sector (Hansen, 1997[50]; OECD, 2017[44]). Public sector employment often offers greater access to family-friendly working arrangements, and sometimes also pays comparatively high wages for low-skilled jobs (Gornick and Jacobs, 1998[51]) – but the prevailing wage structure is more compressed than in private sector employment (Mandel, 2011[52]; Hansen, 1997[50]). Also, gender differences in the positioning of men's and women's jobs in the occupational hierarchy play an important role in the persistent gender pay gaps (Mósesdóttir et al., 2006[53]). Gender pay gaps for top earners in Nordic countries are on par or wider than gender pay gaps for high earners in Canada, France, Italy and the United States (OECD, 2017[21]). In all, gender pay gaps persist, and for a large part these pay differences are related to employment outcomes and characteristics as described above. However, some part of the gender pay differentials remain "unexplained" and may in part reflect discriminatory workplace practices. However, this unexplained part seems smaller than in most OECD countries (Lønkommissionen, 2010[54]; Medlingsinstitutet, 2017[55]; OECD, 2017[56]; OECD, 2017[21]).

2.2.1. Paid, unpaid work and egalitarian attitudes

A disproportionate responsibility for unpaid work limits women's opportunities to enter and progress in the labour market, and across the OECD, women on average engage in more unpaid work than men. This is no different in the Nordic counties, though gaps are noticeably smaller than elsewhere. Figure 2.2 shows that across countries, at the aggregate level, women are more likely to participate in paid work when their male partners take on more housework. In Norway and Sweden gender gaps in unpaid work are smaller than one hour per day (*OECD Gender Data Portal*) which goes hand in hand with high full-time employment rates, in contrast to Germany and the United Kingdom where more than one in three employed women work part-time (*OECD Employment Database*).

To some extent, access to generous public services (including childcare and elderly care) and modern technology limit the time required for unpaid work for both men and women in the Nordic countries. Egalitarian attitudes also likely play a role, though. Nowadays, Nordic men appear more gender egalitarian in their opinions and behaviours than elsewhere. For example, the European Institute for Gender Equality (EIGE) shows that men in Denmark, Norway and Sweden are more likely than men in much of the rest of Europe to strongly *disagree* with statements like "a father must put his career ahead of looking after his young child" and, at least in Denmark and Sweden, to strongly *agree* with gender-egalitarian statements like "equality between men and women is a fundamental right" (EIGE, 2018[57]). Another example is that fathers and mothers in Nordic countries are at least equally likely to work from home occasionally to help match work and family commitments (OECD, 2016[43]) .

OECD (2017[3]) showed that, at 40%, the proportion of individuals that believe parental leave should be split equally between men and women was higher in the Nordic countries than all other OECD countries except for France and Germany. In Sweden, the share was as high as 60%. It also showed for a small number of countries for which such data was available that fathers with a child of pre-school age want their partners to work about 35 hours per week in Finland and Sweden, while this was just 20-25 hours per week in "part-time work countries" as Germany, the Netherlands and the United Kingdom.

Figure 2.2. A better gender balance in unpaid work associates with smaller gender employment gaps

Mean average minutes per day in unpaid work, by gender, and female employment rates, 15-64 year-olds

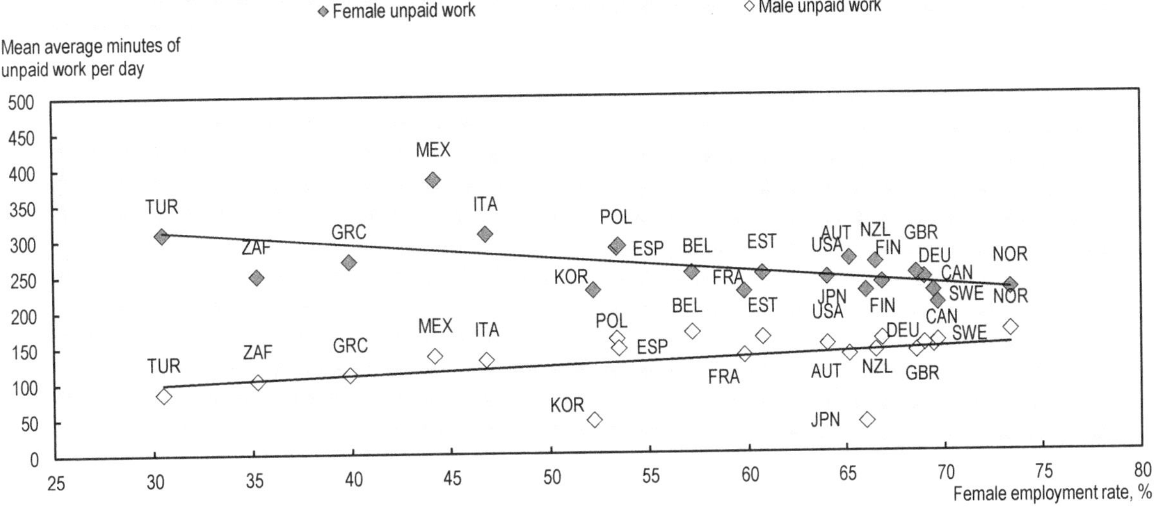

Note: Reference years vary across countries, but concern the period 2009-2016. For more information see the *OECD Gender Data Portal* (http://www.oecd.org/gender/data/).
Source: *OECD Gender Data Portal* (http://www.oecd.org/gender/data/) and *OECD Employment Database* (http://www.oecd.org/employment/emp/onlineoecdemploymentdatabase.htm).

2.3. The overall Nordic social policy stance

Gender policy does not operate in a vacuum, but within an overall policy stance and its impact is related to the prevailing labour market institutions. The policy approach in the Nordic countries involves a comprehensive social policy model that aims to provide universal health and social protection, education and labour market supports. The policy model also involves a large public sector – employing many women – delivering a wide range of public services. Furthermore, the vast majority of workers is covered by collective bargaining between employers and unions, even though union density has been declining since the turn of the century (*OECD Employment Database*).[2]

Broadly speaking, the Nordic social model is characterised by the provision of widely accessible and well-co-ordinated municipal education, employment, family and health services. Public social expenditure comes to around 25-30% of GDP, compared to 21% on average across the OECD (Figure 2.3, Panel A).

Figure 2.3. The Nordic public model is more comprehensive than in most other OECD countries

Panel A: Total public social expenditure as % of GDP, all branches and types of expenditure, 2016 or latest available

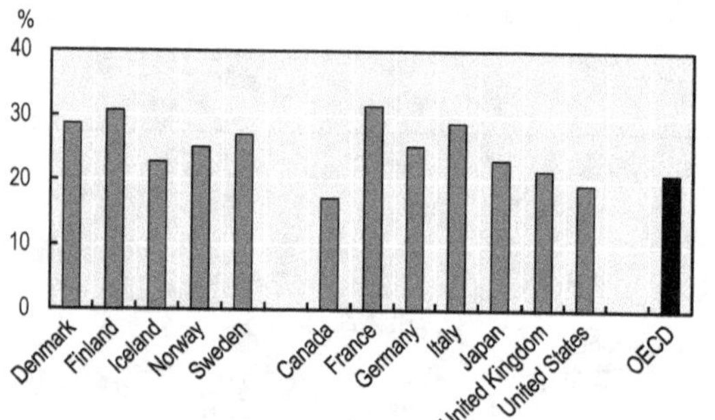

Panel B: Total tax revenue as % of GDP, all levels of government, 2016 or latest available

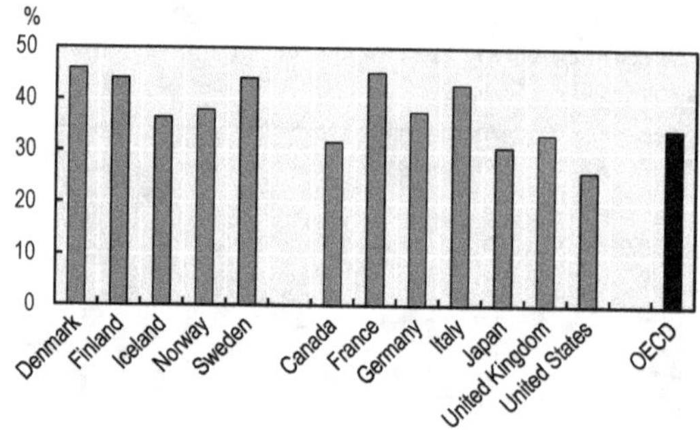

Panel C: Redistributive effect of taxes and transfers, working-age population (18-65), 2015 or latest available

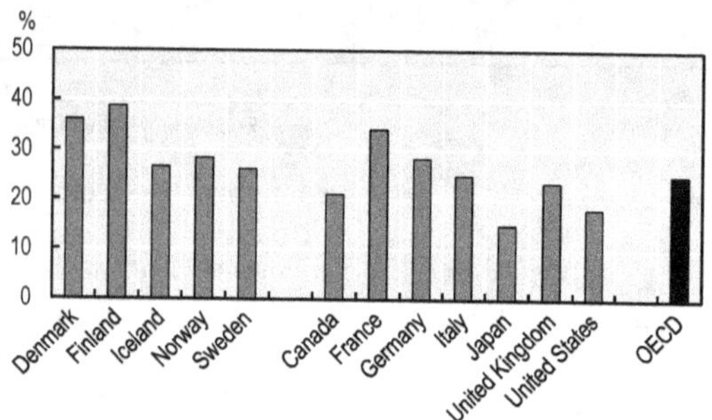

Panel D: Poverty rate after taxes and transfers, total population, 2015 or latest available

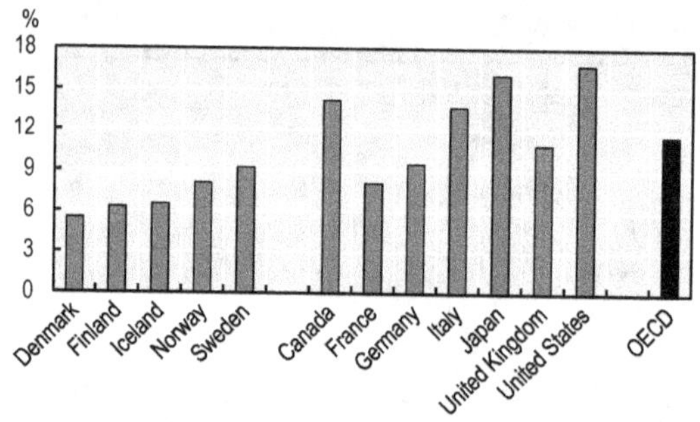

Notes: *Panel A*: data for Japan refer to 2013 and for Canada and Iceland to 2015. Data for Iceland included include public and mandatory private (notably benefits accruing from compulsory occupational pension saving) social expenditure; *Panel B*: data for Japan refer to 2015; *Panel C:* The redistributive effect of taxes and transfers is measured as the difference between the Gini coefficient on market income and the Gini coefficient on disposable income (market income plus cash benefits minus income taxes), divided by the Gini coefficient on market income. Data for Japan refer to 2012 and to 2014 for Denmark, Iceland, Germany and Italy; and, *Panel D*: the relative poverty line is set at 50% of the national median equivalised disposable income (market income plus cash benefits minus income taxes). Data for Japan refer to 2012 and to 2014 for Denmark, Iceland, Germany and Italy.

Sources: *OECD Revenue Statistics* (http://www.oecd.org/tax/tax-policy/revenue-statistics-comparable-tax-revenue-data.htm), *OECD Social Expenditure Database* (http://www.oecd.org/social/expenditure.htm), and *OECD Income Distribution Database* (http://www.oecd.org/social/income-distribution-database.htm).

The model does not come cheap and tax burdens are considerable (OECD, 2017[58]). In 2016, total tax revenue (including social security contributions) amounted to around 45% of GDP in Denmark, Finland and Sweden – about 10 percentage points above the OECD average (Figure 2.3, Panel B). High tax rates may, however, be acceptable to many in the Nordic countries, as it is broadly realised that, in return comes an entitlement to a range of good quality public services, including active labour market policies and family supports such pre-schools and other family services.

Furthermore, the public model is not as expensive as it may appear at first. Nordic countries claw back direct and indirect tax on benefit payments and the associated consumption to the tune of about 4 to 6.5% of GDP in Denmark, Finland, Norway and Sweden (*OECD Social Expenditure Database*). They also do not rely on voluntary private social spending (e.g. health care and pensions) or associated tax support as, for example in the United States. When these effects are taken into account, total social spending in Nordic countries is below that in France and the United States (see (Adema, Fron and Ladaique, 2011[59]) for the underlying methodology).

Tax levels do not just affect financing and levels of social spending but the design of tax/benefit systems also determines it redistributive nature. Figure 2.3, Panel C compares the degree of income inequality in countries before and after accounting for taxes and transfers, and shows that the tax/benefit systems in the Nordic counties are more redistributive than in most OECD countries (OECD, 2015[11]; Pareliussen et al., 2018[60]), even though the redistributive power of Nordic tax/benefit systems has weakened in recent years (Causa and Hermansen, 2017[61]; Pedersen and Kuhnle, 2017[26]). Furthermore, these indicators likely underestimate the redistributive power of Nordic country systems as they do not account for the redistributive effect deriving from the provision of public services financed out of general tax revenue (Adema, Fron and Ladaique, 2014[62]). Both the redistributive nature of the tax/benefit system and the high male and female employment rates - as facilitated by public ECEC-services - contribute to the relative low poverty rates in Nordic countries (Figure 2.3, Panel D).

2.4. How did we get here? The development of family and gender-equality policy in the Nordic countries

All OECD countries provide gender equality policies in at least some form, though the types and intensity of support offered differs. Differences in countries' histories, labour markets, attitudes towards families and gender norms, the role of government, and the relative weight given to the various underlying policy objectives all mean that each have historically taken and continue to take their own approach to family and gender policy (see, for example, Thévenon (2011[22]) and Adema (2012[23]) for a discussion and overview). The Nordic approach to family and gender-equality policy grew largely out of the wider Nordic welfare model (see above), and especially its core principles of "work friendliness" and full participation (Kuhnle and Hort, 2004[24]; Pedersen and Kuhnle, 2017[26]). The various gender equality interventions are closely linked and interdependent, geared towards the same goal: making it easier for men and women to fully engage in the labour market.

Industrialisation in the Nordic countries started around the 1870s and was spurred on by free trade for export-based goods and manufacturing industry (Iqbal and Todi, 2015[63]). During the initial phase of industrialisation - from the 1870s up to the First World War (WWI) - it was common for women to leave the labour market upon marriage to take care of the household and raise children (as is still common in Asian OECD countries, for example). After WWI, policy started to develop non-discrimination legislation and other initiatives that facilitate widespread female employment participation. For example, in 1921, Denmark adopted a law on equal access to employment for men and women (Danmarks Statistik, 2015[64]) while in 1939 Sweden became one of the first countries in Europe to introduce legislation prohibiting dismissal from employment on the grounds of marriage or parenthood (Hilson, 2007[1]; Statistics Sweden, 2016[2]). Today, all Nordic countries have laws mandating equal pay for work of equal value. They also have extensive legal protection against discrimination in the labour market, legislation against sexual harassment both at work and in wider society (Bladini, 2017[65]; NIKK, 2018[66]), and, to slightly differing extents, rules covering the representation of men and women in the media, such as through the regulation of gender-discriminatory advertising, for instance (Kosunen et al., 2017[67]).

A major step forward came with changes to the Nordic income tax systems during the years between the late-1950s and 1970s. Historically, the Nordic countries operated joint taxation systems, meaning that second earners (typically the female partner) were effectively taxed at the same rate as their (often higher-earning) spouses (usually the male partner). This pushed up marginal tax rates for second earners, providing strong incentives to stay at home. Financial incentives to work for second earners increased with the individualisation of tax systems: in 1959 in Norway, 1971 in Denmark and Sweden, and later on during in the 1970s in Iceland and Finland. Nowadays, tax/benefit systems in Nordic countries favour dual-earner families over one-earner couple families (*OECD Family Database*). Participation tax rates (see notes to Figure 2.4) for second earners in couple families are low in international comparison in Norway and Sweden (Figure 2.4), and close to the OECD average in other Nordic countries. The high average tax rates on second earners in Denmark, Finland and Iceland may contribute to an income effect on female labour supply, while failing to use childcare supports is like throwing away a highly subsidised good: these two factors help explain the high rate of female labour force participation (OECD, 2002[68]). Tax/benefit systems in Nordic countries generally do not stimulate part-time employment.

Employers in Nordic countries are encouraged to actively promote gender equality and prevent discrimination. The details of the regulations vary, but in Sweden, for example, employers must develop guidelines to prevent sexual harassment and carry out annual salary assessments. These salary assessments must include transparent wage criteria or bonus schemes to avoid gender discrimination. Employers must also analyse the causes of any discrimination that has come to light and take appropriate action.

Various OECD countries have recently introduced measures to improve pay transparency (OECD, 2017[21]), but Iceland was the first country to introduce a mandatory pay equality certificate. Since 1 June 2017 legislation in Iceland requires companies with 25 or more employees to disclose the gender composition of the workforce and those in management positions (OECD, 2017[56]). The government has developed a certification scheme for gender pay equality to ensure that all jobs of equal value are paid the same, and the certification process has to be undertaken every three years to ensure maintaining standards. The introduction of a mechanism that regularly considers pay practice in companies will maintain a focus on gender pay equality in companies on a recurrent basis. Future evaluations of this and other pay transparency initiatives across the OECD will contribute to enhancing the effectives of such measures with an aim to further reducing gender pay gaps.

Figure 2.4. Participation tax rates are moderate to low in the Nordic OECD countries

Participation tax rate, second earner in a two-earner two-child couple family on 67% of average earnings, 2015

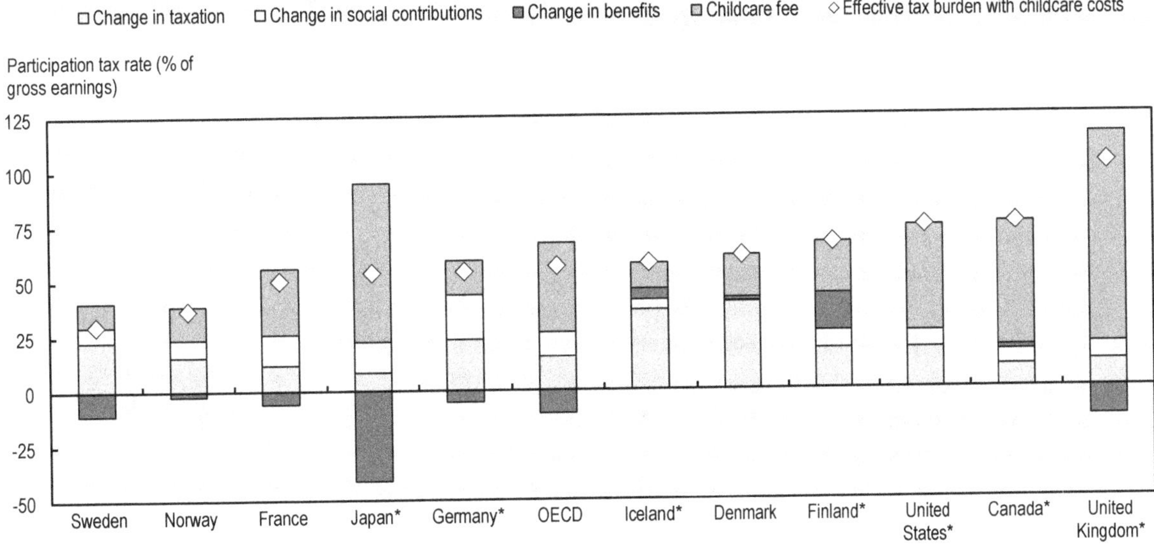

Note: The "participation tax rate" is the proportion of prospective gross earnings that would be "taxed" away through direct taxation (income tax plus social security contributions), reduced out-of-work and income-tested benefits, and out-of-pocket childcare costs, should the individual (in this case the second earner in a two-earner, two-child couple family) enter paid work full-time at 67% of the average wage. The first earner is assumed to be employed full-time earning the average wage. Data for countries marked with an * are based on estimates for a specific region or city, rather than for the country as a whole. See the *OECD Tax and Benefit Systems* website (http://www.oecd.org/els/soc/benefits-and-wages.htm) for more detail.
Source: *OECD Tax and Benefit Systems* (http://www.oecd.org/els/soc/benefits-and-wages.htm).

One of the key features of the Nordic model is the provision of a comprehensive package of family supports. Public spending on family benefits amounts to around 3- 3.5% of GDP in Nordic countries (the OECD average is around 2.5%), about 60% which is delivered in the form of family services including public childcare. On average across the OECD, only 40% of family spending is spent on family services (*OECD Social Expenditure Database*). The specifics vary from country to country, but the general emphasis is on encouraging continuous employment for all parents, including single parents, and promoting a "dual earner-dual carer" family model. Recognising that gender gaps often emerge in full once children arrive, the Nordic countries provide a 'continuum' of support as children grow up. Parents can access generous paid leave when children are very young, followed by a place in subsidised early childhood education and care (ECEC) and out-of-school-hours (OSH) care activities once they enter full-time education. Tax systems encourage paid work by second earners (see above), while paid parental leave systems often encourage fathers and mothers to share care responsibilities by means of individualised "use it or lose it" paid leave entitlements (NIKK, forthcoming[69]).

2.4.1. Developing early childhood education and care systems

ECEC services are central to most family and gender objectives. Affordable and high-equality ECEC provides parents with options to make the work-life decisions that fit their needs and helps parents with young children fully engage in paid work. As it is mothers far more than fathers who adjust their patterns of paid work when children arrive (OECD, 2016[70]; OECD, 2017[21]), ECEC services are especially important for female labour market opportunities and for ensuring that women have the freedom to engage in paid work even after becoming parents (Jaumotte, 2003[71]; Thévenon, 2013[72]; Del Boca, 2015[73]; Olivetti and Petrongolo, 2017[74]).

ECEC systems and policies differ greatly between countries. All OECD governments support and help fund early childhood education and care in one way or another, but the scale of support and means and methods of delivering assistance are diverse. Some OECD countries, (e.g. Australia, the Netherlands and the United Kingdom), rely mostly on the private market for the provision of ECEC services, with cash supports and demand-side subsidies given to parents to help increase affordability. Others, like many of the Baltic and Eastern European OECD countries (e.g. Estonia, Latvia, Hungary), place a lot of weight on public pre-primary services for children above age three, and provide less support for services for very young children aged 0-2.

The Nordic countries operate comprehensive public-supported early childhood education and care systems, covering children from around (and sometimes before) age one, up. Developed with heavy emphasis on helping parents participate in paid work, especially in Denmark and Sweden (Brandth et al., 2012[25]), ECEC services have played a pivotal role in the expansion of women's employment in the Nordic countries over the past few decades (see Section 3.1). Long time-series on children enrolment are unfortunately not available for most of the Nordic countries, but data for Sweden provide a good example of how the two have developed hand-in-hand. In 1965, for instance, employment rates for women aged 25-54 were as low as around 55% while at the same time only 3% of children aged 0 to 6 were enrolled in formal childcare (OECD, 2005[30]). Enrolment rates increased rapidly since, however, to 50% of all children age 0 to 6 by 1985, and have been around 75% since the mid-2000s (Figure 2.5). Similarly, for Denmark the enrolment rates among 3-year-olds increased from 35% in 1973 to 60% in 1985 and 75% in 1995 (OECD, 2002[68]). Today, 97% of 3-year-olds in Denmark are enrolled in ECEC programmes (OECD, 2017[75]).

Figure 2.5. Formal childcare in Sweden developed alongside increasing female employment

Childcare enrolment rate, 0-6 year-olds, and female employment rates, 25-54 year-olds, Sweden, 1965-2016

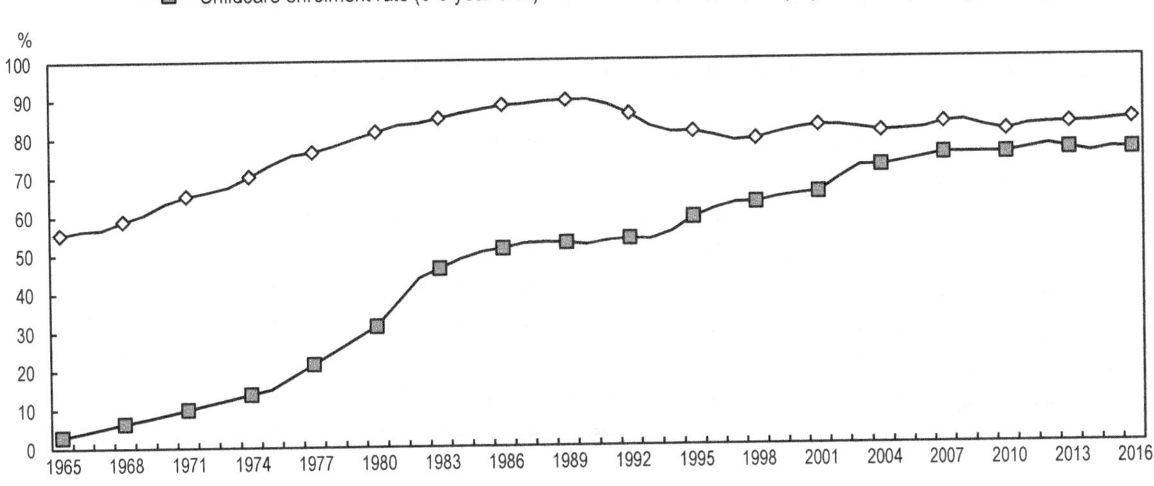

Source: For the female employment rate: *OECD Employment Database* (http://www.oecd.org/employment/emp/onlineoecdemploymentdatabase.htm); for the childcare enrolment rate: data provided by the Swedish authorities for 1965-2002, and *NOSOSCO Database* (http://nowbase.org/da) and NOSOSCO (2017), *Social Protection in the Nordic Countries 2015/2016, Nordic Social Statistical Committee* (http://norden.diva-portal.org/smash/get/diva2:1148493/FULLTEXT02.pdf), for 2003-2016.

Participation in ECEC facilities is largely financed through general taxation, and regardless of their structure, ECEC facilities must follow early childhood- and teaching requirements decided at the national level. Fees are heavily subsidised, with services often available at reduced-rates or, in some countries (e.g. Denmark), free for low-income families. Support generally covers full-time participation (around 6 hours per day). Only Norway has a "cash-for-care" benefit (see below) that facilitates use of ECEC facilities on a part-time basis.

Participation in ECEC services is highest in Denmark where two out of three 0-2 year olds are enrolled in such services, and over 95% of all 3-5 year olds in Denmark, Iceland, Norway and Sweden participate in ECEC services (Figure 2.6). Participation rates for 0-2 year olds also depend on the duration of parental leave benefits (see Section 2.4.2), but are well above the OECD average. The exception is Finland, where the widespread use of the state-funded home care allowance means more parents than in the other Nordics care for children at home until they reach age 3 (see Section 2.4.2).

Figure 2.6. Participation in formal child- and out-of-school hours care is more widespread in Nordic countries than elsewhere

Panel A. Participation rates for 0-2 year-olds in formal childcare and pre-school services and for 3-5 year-olds in pre-primary education or primary school, 2014 or latest year available

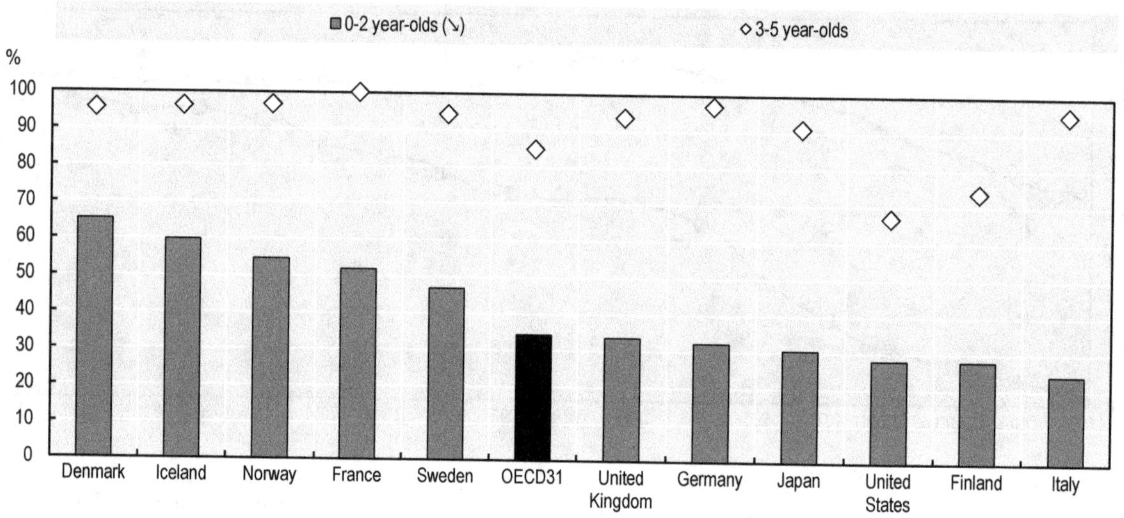

Panel B. Participation rates for 6-11 year-olds in centre-based out-of-school-hours care services, 2014 or latest year available

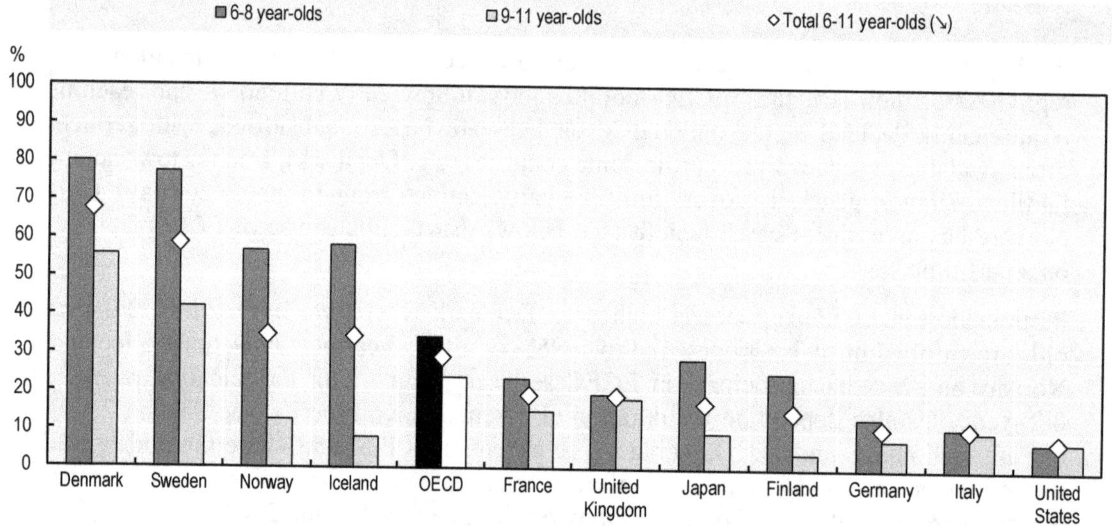

Note: See *OECD Family Database*, indicators PF3.2 and PF 4.3 for more detail and country-specific notes.
Source: *OECD Family Database* Indicators PF3.2 and PF4.3 (http://www.oecd.org/els/family/database.htm).

But childcare needs do not end when children enter primary school. Denmark and Sweden in particular have developed comprehensive out-of-school hours care supports. Rules on participation by age-groups differ (NOSOSCO, 2016[76]), but in general participation tails off when children enter their teens (Figure 2.6).

2.4.2. Leave to care for children

Paid leave policies have become a major feature of family and gender policy in most OECD countries in recent decades. On top of protecting the health of working mothers and their new-born children, paid leave helps keep mothers in paid employment and provides parents with the opportunity to spend time at home with children when they are young (Adema, Clarke and Frey, 2015[77]; Rossin-Slater, 2017[78]).

In all Nordic countries, both mothers and fathers are entitled to paid parental leave, although the design of the national parental leave benefits varies from country to country. In 2016, Sweden had the longest period of paid parental leave in the Nordic countries (69 weeks) and Iceland the shortest (39). In Denmark, Finland and Norway, the period of paid parental leave is around one year, though in Denmark and Norway the duration can be extended slightly (by 8-14 and 10 weeks, respectively) in exchange for a proportional reduction in the payment rate (NOSOSCO, 2016[76]). In addition, both Finland (until a child's third birthday) and Norway (for children between 1 and 2 years of age) provide "home care" or "cash-for-care" allowances to parents who do not use public childcare services. Home care allowance payment rates are nowhere near those of parental leave - in Finland, the average payment in 2015 was EUR 419 per month (Blum, Koslowski and Moss, 2017[79]), equivalent to about 12% of average gross earnings - but still provide second-earners in couple families (usually the mother) with strong financial incentives to stay at home and not engage in paid work, in particular if they would earn low wages. Indeed, very long periods of leave like these may undo many of the positive effects of paid leave on female employment and hamper women's earnings and career progression (Thévenon and Solaz, 2013[80]; Adema, Clarke and Frey, 2015[77]).

In order to promote gender equality, both at home and in the labour market, efforts have been made to encourage parents to divide leave entitlements equally, either by means of ensuring high payment rates of income support during leave and/or by providing both fathers *and* mothers with their own individual paid leave entitlements on a "use it or lose it" basis. Across the Nordic countries payment rates during parental leave are high. Estimates from NOSOSCO, for example, suggest a couple family with a new-born and two other children with earnings at 175% of the average wage can expect a disposable income of 75 to 89% of previous household income when the second earner takes parental leave (NOSOSCO, 2016[76]).

All of the Nordic countries provide fathers with their own individual non-transferable entitlements to paid leave, either through paid paternity leave or through the use of "mother and father quotas" in parental leave systems – that is, non-transferable periods of parental leave that are reserved for each parent respectively. Norway was the first to introduce such a quota in 1993, followed by Sweden in 1995, and Finland[3] and Iceland in the early-2000s. Denmark also introduced a father quota in 1997, but this was later abolished in 2002 in a broad reform of leave arrangement that included abolition of "childminding leave" that could be used for prolonged periods (OECD, 2002[68]; Brandth et al., 2012[25]). In 2016, among the Nordic countries, Sweden provided the longest entitlement to fathers-only paid leave (a three-month father quota, plus ten days of paid paternity leave), followed by Iceland (a three-month father quota), Norway (a ten-week father quota) and Finland (a nine-week fathers-only paid leave) (Figure 2.7). Denmark provides fathers with two weeks paid paternity leave.

Figure 2.7. In most Nordic countries, two to three months of paid child-related leave are reserved for fathers

Duration of paid paternity leave and paid parental leave reserved for fathers, in weeks, 2016

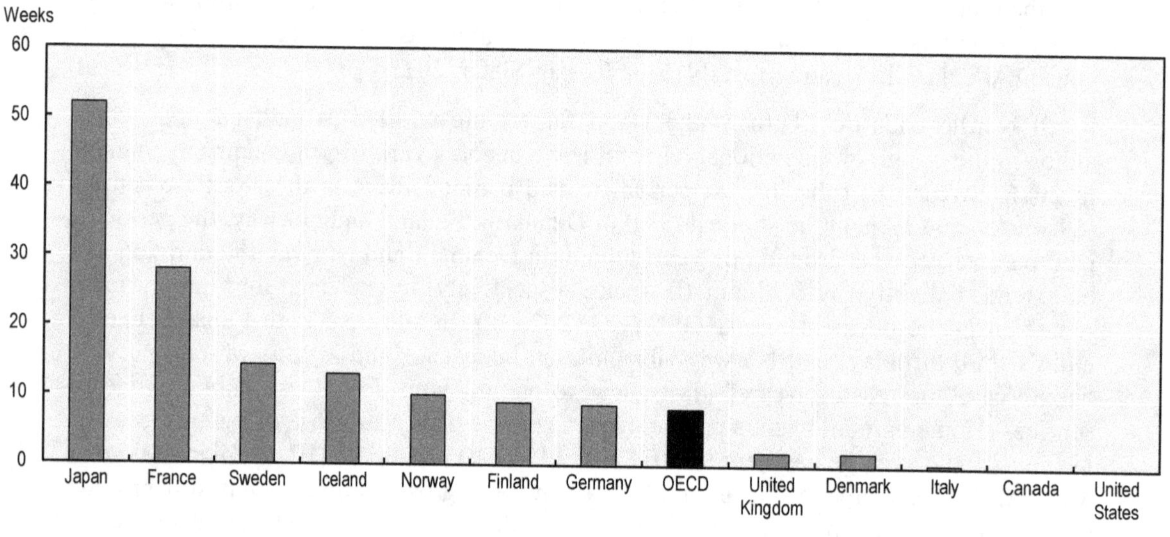

Note: Information refers to entitlements to paid paternity leave, "father quotas" or periods of parental leave that can be used only by the father and cannot be transferred to the mother, and any weeks of paid sharable leave that must be taken by the father in order for the family to qualify for 'bonus' weeks of parental leave. Data refer to entitlements in place as of April 2016 and do not reflect entitlements introduced or amended after April 2016. Data reflect statutory entitlements provided at the national or federal level only. They do not include regional variations or additional/alternative entitlements provided by states/provinces or local governments (e.g. Québec in Canada, or California in the United States), or any employer-provided benefits that are paid beyond the statutory minimum duration.
Source: *OECD Family Database* Indicator PF2.1 (http://www.oecd.org/els/family/database.htm).

The introduction of "father quotas" can increase the likelihood of fathers taking leave, especially if well-paid (perhaps around two-thirds or more of last earnings). For example, in Iceland, men's share of all parental leave days taken was just 3% prior to the introduction of the mother and father quotas in the early-2000s; following the reform, this increased to roughly one-third of total days used (Eydal et al., 2015[81]). However, with the unfolding of the economic crisis and the subsequent reduction in payment rates the intensity with which fathers in Iceland used parent leave declined, especially among low-income fathers, while mothers started using mother leave for longer periods (Sigurdardottir and Garðarsdóttir, 2018[82]).

Over the past 15 years fathers in the Nordic countries have started to use more of their parental leave. Indeed, Icelandic and Swedish fathers are among the most likely in the OECD to take paid child-related leave. In 2015, fathers in Iceland and Sweden took close to 30% of all parental leave days, while those in Norway took roughly 20% and in Denmark about 10% (NOSOSCO, 2016[76]). This is higher than in France and Japan, where eligible fathers can access paid leave for six and 12 months, respectively (Figure 2.7). However, less than 5 % of eligible fathers use these benefits as in France payment rates are low (about one-sixth of average earnings) and in Japan many fathers in regular employment are reluctant to take so as not to jeopardize their career prospects (*OECD Family Database*).

Despite these developments, mothers still remain the dominant users of sharable parental leave and home-care benefits. Moving towards fully-individualised paid parental leave systems – with both mothers and fathers receiving identical, non-transferable entitlements to paid leave and any sharable elements abolished entirely – could encourage fathers to take more paid leave and could help generate a better sharing of paid and unpaid work, in turn generating a number of benefits for parents and families (OECD, 2017[21]). These include benefits for child health and development, for fathers' well-being, and, especially relevant here, for women's careers (OECD, 2017[21]). For instance, on top of reducing women's unpaid work burdens, the social normalisation of leave taking by fathers may help reduce gender discrimination in the workplace and reduce the risk that women are the only ones taking care-related leave – and with it the subsequent negative effects on female earnings and career advancements (Rønsen and Kitterød, 2015[83]).

On top of entitlements to paid leave, working parents in some of the Nordic countries can also reduce working hours when children are young (Blum, Koslowski and Moss, 2017[79]). In Sweden, for example, employees with children under eight years of age can reduce their weekly working hours by 25% and/or take part-time paid parental leave. Parents in Finland have a right to work part time and those in Norway a right to request a part-time work schedule, though in both countries the new working schedule is subject to negotiation between employers and employees, and employers can deny request in case of compelling business reasons. Parents in Denmark and Iceland are not legally entitled to part-time work or flexible work arrangements. However, in Denmark, parents can request flexible arrangements upon return from parental leave, while in Iceland employers are required to take measures to help employees combine work and family life.

3. Progress and the pay-off: How investment in gender equality in the Nordic countries have contributed to economic growth

There are several ways in which improving women's economic opportunities could lead to better economic performance. First and most obviously, allowing and encouraging women to engage in the labour market is likely to boost output by increasing the supply of labour. Across the OECD, workers are a key productive asset – indeed, in almost all, labour still contributes the bulk of national production (OECD, 2015[84]) – and adding more workers to the labour force should lead to more output.

On top of this, however, there are a number of additional routes through which gender equality can influence growth. Making better use of female workers could lead to productivity gains, for example, perhaps by improving job match, or by making more efficient use of the available talent pool. Increasing women's economic power could also lead to improved consumption and savings behaviours, at least in the context of less-developed countries (Stotsky, 2006[85]). Encouraging women to work more is likely to come with costs, especially in terms of a decrease in unpaid domestic work, which, if properly accounted for, would contribute substantially to national production (OECD, 2016[34]). However, even here there may still be net welfare gains, if goods and services previously supplied by unpaid workers (like childcare and elder care) are produced more efficiently outside the home than within it. All these mechanisms can play an important role, but due to data and methodological issues the focus of this section falls largely on the first mechanism mentioned – the contribution of women's labour input (in numbers and hours work) to economic performance.

The aim of the section is to measure the economic gains from the promotion of gender equality in the Nordic countries. It seeks to address two main questions: first, to what extent have changes in women's labour input contributed to past economic growth in the Nordic countries; and second, how much do Nordic countries continue to gain from their current relatively high levels of female employment and gender equality in the labour market? To do so, it draws together historical time-series on macro-economic performance and women's employment, and combines them with growth accounting (Box 3.1) and development accounting (Annex B) techniques. The overarching objective is to capture and quantify how much the Nordic economies have benefited (and are still benefiting) from their comparatively gender-equal labour markets and high levels of female employment.

There are some limits to this exercise that are important to state at the outset. The estimates shown here do not account for the impact of any changes in female paid work on unpaid work and household production, for instance. As a result, they may possibly overstate the boost to actual living standards enjoyed by households following an increase in female employment. They also do not account for any gender differences in productivity, and implicitly assume that one additional hour of labour input produces exactly the same output regardless of sex, age, education, and so on. This assumption is largely unavoidable, because of a lack of adequate time-series data disaggregated by at least sex and age that could be used to capture worker productivity. Nonetheless, it should be kept in mind when interpreting estimates of the amounts of economic growth or output that can be accounted for by a certain group of workers.

Box 3.1. Measuring the contribution of changes in women's employment to economic growth using growth accounting

Much of the analysis in this section is based on growth accounting – a procedure used to identify and decompose the sources of economic growth. A detailed overview of the procedure is given in Annex B, but the basic idea is to use information on observed trends in macroeconomic indicators to split growth into its main components parts – that is, under standard macroeconomic theory, into labour, capital, and total factor productivity (Solow, 1956[86]). Data permitting, the contribution of each of these main components can then be further decomposed into their own sub-components. For example, the contribution of labour input to growth can be split between changes in employment in the different sectors of the economy, while the contribution of capital can be divided between ICT-related capital (e.g. computer hardware, telecommunications equipment, and computer software) and non-ICT capital (more traditional forms of capital, like machinery and transport equipment).

In this report, the focus is on the contribution of labour input to growth and, in particular, on the contribution of women's labour input. Growth accounting is used to identify and separate the contribution of labour from the other two main components – capital and total factor productivity, from here on labelled together as "labour productivity" – and then to decompose the contribution of labour input itself. Labour input is, in this instance, separated into three parts: changes in the size of the working-age population, the employment rate, and, where data allow, average hours worked per employed person. The contribution of the size of the working-age population is separated out first, to capture and control for the effects of shifts in demographic structure. The contributions of changes in both the employment rate and average working hours are then decomposed by gender and, where possible, by age group too. The latter two factors (the employment rate and average working hours) are where the main interest lies – they provide information on the extent to which changes in men's and especially women's employment rates and working hours have contributed to economic growth.

3.1. Gains in female employment have made large contributions to Nordic economic growth

Many OECD countries have made progress on narrowing gender employment gaps over the past few decades (OECD, 2017[21]), but the Nordic countries started earlier and moved faster than most. Even as early as the mid-1980s, the five Nordic OECD members could boast that at least two-thirds of working-age women (15-64) were in paid employment (Figure 3.1, Panel A). At this time in countries like France, less than half of all working-age women were employed (Figure 3.1, Panel B). In Italy, it was roughly one-third.

Much of the growth in female employment in the Nordic countries took place in the years prior to 1990 (Figure 3.1, Panel A). Female employment rates were already fairly high in the Nordic countries in the 1960s (Figure 3.1, Panel A), but further major gains were made across especially the 1970s and 1980s. In Sweden, for example, the employment rate for working-age women grew from 52.8% to 81.0% over the two-and-a-half decades between 1965 and 1990 – an average rate of increase of more than one percentage point per year (Figure 3.1, Panel A). By comparison, in both France and the United Kingdom, the working-age female employment rate increased by only around 20 percentage points over the *five* decades between 1965 and 2015 (Figure 3.1, Panels B and C). Denmark and Iceland also made large gains in female employment during the decades prior to 1990 – although for these two countries we must rely on estimated data (see Annex B) – as did Norway, at least in the years since consistent records began in 1972 (Figure 3.1, Panel A). Gains were slightly smaller in Finland, largely because female employment was already very high in the 1960s. Nonetheless, even there, the working-age female employment rate still increased by 10 percentage points between 1970 and 1990 (Figure 3.1, Panel A).

Employment gains in the Nordic countries slowed after 1990 (Figure 3.1, Panel A), as the economic crisis in the early 1990s led to large employment losses for women as well as for men (Figure A A.1. Panel A). In Finland and Sweden working-age female employment rates fell by around 12-13 percentage points from their highest points in 1990 to their lowest in 1994 and 1998, respectively (Figure 3.1, Panel A). Female employment has stablished and recovered slightly since, but gains have been much smaller and slower than those seen prior to 1990 (Figure 3.1, Panel A). Iceland has seen the largest increase in working-age female employment since 1990, at 8 percentage points.

Despite the slow-down, current female employment levels remain high in the Nordic countries. Female employment rates in Finland and Sweden are still slightly lower than their pre-crisis peaks (Figure 3.1, Panel A) but, taking a wider perspective, women in the Nordic countries remain far more likely to be found in paid employment today than they were four or five decades ago. In Denmark, Iceland, Norway and Sweden, working-age female employment rates are currently about 20-25 percentage points higher than in the 1960s or early-1970s. Finland has seen smaller gains but, even so, the working-age female employment rate is still about 6 percentage points higher than in 1970.

The gains made on female employment by the Nordic countries have provided a considerable boost to economic growth over the past half century. Figure 3.2 summarises results from a first growth accounting exercise, with growth in GDP per capita decomposed into parts that can be accounted for by changes in: labour productivity, the working-age share of the population, and male and female headcount employment (see Box 3.1). This first exercise covers the contribution of headcount employment only, with changes in working hours left out for the time being (see Section 3.2 and Box 3.2). Some caution should be used when comparing across countries, as differences in the length of available time-series mean estimates are not fully comparable.

Figure 3.1. The Nordic countries have seen large increases in female employment over the past 50 years, but growth has slowed

Female employment rate, 15-64 year-olds, 1960-2016, selected OECD countries

Panel A. Nordic OECD member countries

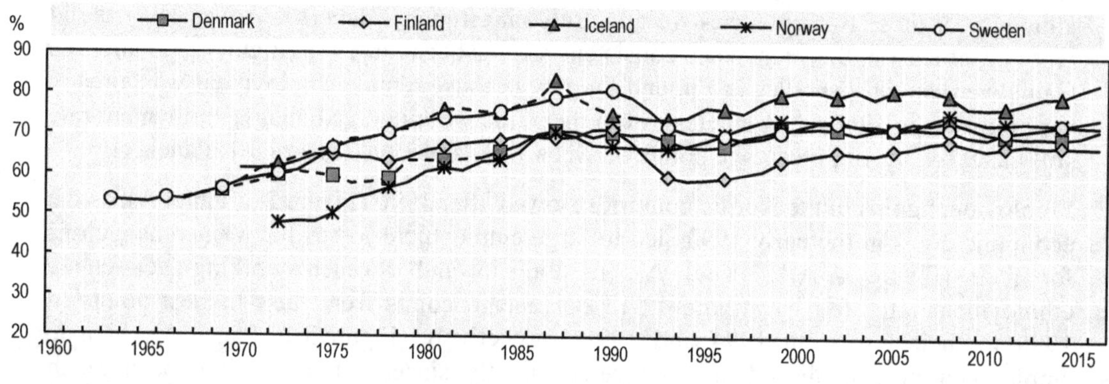

Panel B. Selected other OECD member countries

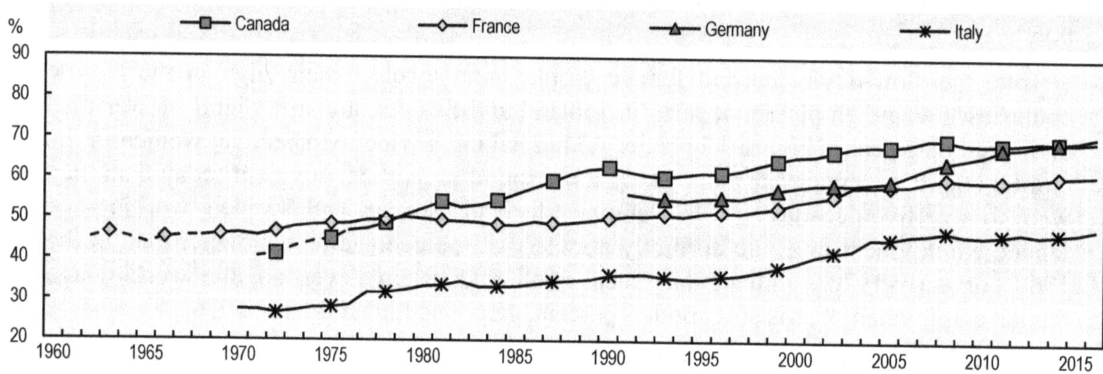

Panel C. Selected other OECD member countries (cont.)

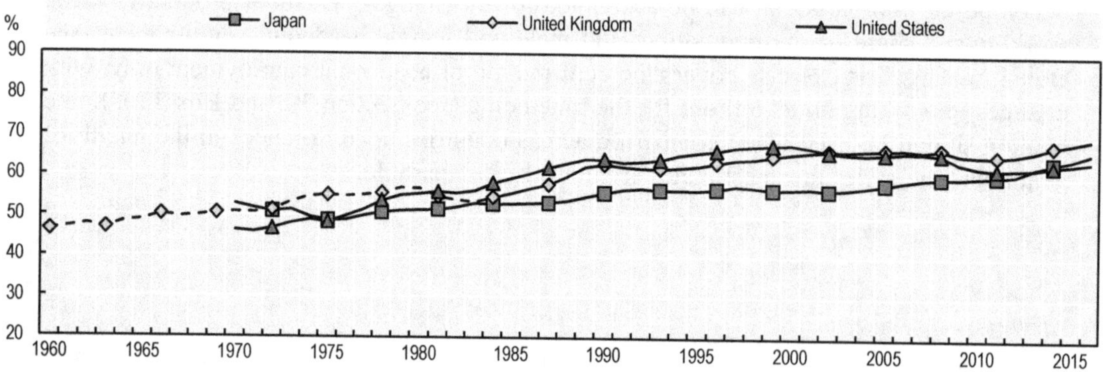

Note: Dashed lines reflect estimated data points (see Annex B).
Source: *OECD Employment Database* (http://www.oecd.org/employment/emp/onlineoecdemploymentdatabase.htm), and OECD estimates based on data from the *OECD Annual Labour Force Statistics Database* (http://stats.oecd.org/index.aspx?queryid=451), Eurostat (http://ec.europa.eu/eurostat/data/database), and national statistical offices (see Annex B).

Figure 3.2. Except for in Finland, gains in female employment account for between 10% and 20% of average annual growth in the Nordic countries

Average annual rate of growth in GDP per capita and disaggregation of growth into its primary components, longest available series, Nordic and selected other OECD member countries

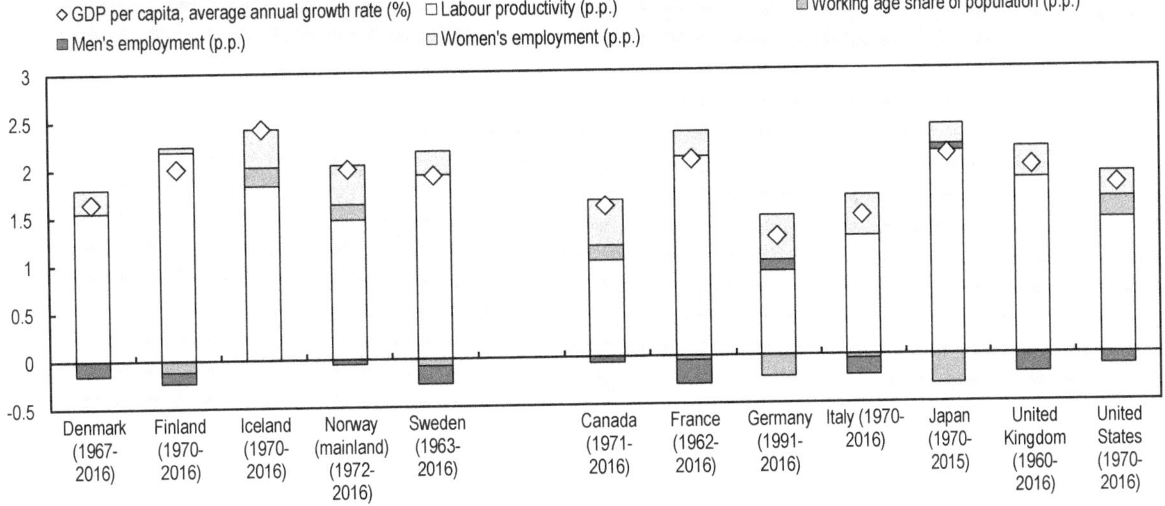

Note: Estimates based on the decomposition of national accounts data using labour force survey estimates. Differences in the time periods covered mean estimates are not fully comparable across countries. See Annex B for more detail.

Source: OECD estimates based on data from the *OECD National Accounts Database* (http://www.oecd.org/std/na/), the *OECD Employment Database* (http://www.oecd.org/employment/emp/onlineoecdemploymentdatabase.htm), the European Commission's *AMECO Database* (http://ec.europa.eu/economy_finance/ameco/user/serie/SelectSerie.cfm), *Eurostat* (http://ec.europa.eu/eurostat/data/database), and national statistical offices (see Annex B).

Labour productivity gains (covering growth linked to both capital and technological progress) account for the bulk of economic growth across all twelve of the OECD countries included in Figure 3.2. This is consistent with a number of existing studies (Scarpetta et al., 2000[87]; Duval and de la Maisonneuve, 2010[88]; Johansson et al., 2013[89]) that find that technology in particular accounts for the largest part of recent economic growth in OECD countries.

Figure 3.2 suggests that, except for in Finland, gains in female employment account for around 10-20% of all growth in GDP per capita in the Nordic countries over the past 40-50 years (Figure 3.2). In Iceland and Norway[4], approximately 0.40 percentage points of the average annual rate of GDP per capita growth over recent decades can be linked to gains in female employment, while in Denmark and Sweden this is about 0.25 percentage points (Figure 3.2). Gains are relatively small in Finland, as the female employment rate was already at a high level at the start of the period examined (1970).

Box 3.2. Summary of the data used in the growth accounting exercise

Data sources used for the growth accounting exercise

The data used for the growth accounting exercise is taken from national accounts databases and supplemented by estimates based on information from labour force surveys (Annex B). Data for the first stage of the process, which involves decomposing growth into its main components like capital and total labour input, are taken from the *OECD National Accounts Database*. The data series used include Gross Domestic Product (GDP), total population, total employment, and average working hours per person employed. On occasion important series are missing in the OECD database. Where this is the case, values are filled or interpolated using information from alternative national accounts databases, such as the European Commission's *AMECO Database* or those published by national statistical offices.

The second stage of the growth accounting exercise, which involves decomposing the contributions of the employment rate and average working hours by gender and age group, requires data on population, employment, and working hours that are disaggregated by age and gender. National accounts databases do not typically provide breakdowns by age or gender, so these data are estimated using information from labour force surveys. Details of this procedure are given in Annex B but, in short, it involves splitting and allocating the overall population, employment, and hours-worked totals from national accounts databases according to information on the distribution of the given series provided by labour force survey data. The labour force survey data are taken primarily from the *OECD Employment Database* or from data series supplied by the Nordic national statistical offices in response to an OECD questionnaire. Where data are missing, values are filled using information from alternative sources such as the Eurostat database or alternative information from national statistical offices, or are estimated by trending the nearest observation back or forward using alternative but similar series. More detail is given in Annex B.

Time period covered by the growth accounting exercise

The time period covered by the growth accounting exercise is limited by data availability and varies across countries. Generally, for this exercise, a longer time-series is preferable to a shorter one. Shorter time-series starting in, say, the 1980s or 1990s are likely to miss much of the growth of female employment, and therefore much of the contribution of women's employment to economic growth. However, consistent and comparable time-series going back to the 1960s or 1970s are not always available; labour force survey data disaggregated by age and gender are usually the biggest constraint, with data on working hours especially scarce. In the best cases the relevant measures are available right through from the early-1960s to 2016.

To maximise the time period covered, several sets of estimates are produced, each progressively more detailed but also more constrained in terms of the period covered. The first set (shown in Figure 3.2 and in Table A A.3) covers the contribution of changes in the employment rate by gender, only; the second (shown in Table A A.4) covers the contribution of changes in the employment-to-population rate by gender and also age group; and the last set (shown in Figure 3.5 and in Table A A.5) adds in the contribution of changes in average working hours by gender. Table 3.1 summarises the time period covered for each country under each set of estimates.

Table 3.1. The time period covered varies across countries and estimates

Summary of time period covered by the different estimates, by country

		Employment rate, by gender (Figure 3.2)	Employment rate, by gender and age (Table A A.4)	Employment rate and average working hours, by gender (Figure 3.5)
Nordic OECD member countries	Denmark	1967-2016	1983-2016	1983-2016
	Finland	1970-2016	1970-2016	1990-2016
	Iceland	1970-2016	1991-2016	1991-2016
	Norway	1972-2016	1972-2016	1975-2016
	Sweden	1963-2016	1963-2016	1987-2016
Selected other OECD member countries	Canada	1971-2016	1976-2016	1976-2016
	France	1962-2016	1968-2016	1983-2016
	Germany	1991-2016	1991-2016	1991-2016
	Italy	1970-2016	1970-2016	1983-2016
	Japan	1970-2016	1970-2016	-
	United Kingdom	1960-2016	1984-2016	1984-2016
	United States	1970-2016	1970-2016	1979-2016

How important are these contributions? It is difficult to know exactly what the Nordic economies would have looked like if female employment had not grown over the past few decades, and it is too simple to say that the average growth rate in, say, Denmark would have been 0.25 percentage points lower if women's employment had simply stagnated. Male employment and hours might have responded to pick up the slack, for example, or perhaps labour productivity would have contributed even more. Nonetheless, to put these numbers in context, removing the contribution of women's employment from the actual observed rate of growth would mean current GDP per capita would be around USD 5 000-6 000 (2010 PPP) smaller in Denmark and Sweden, USD 7 500 smaller in Iceland, and almost USD 9 000 smaller in Norway (mainland). Even in Finland, where gains in female employment have contributed only roughly 0.05 percentage points to average annual growth, GDP per capita would still be roughly USD 1 500 smaller if it was not for the parts of growth accounted for by changes in female employment. These are big numbers. They equate to losses of roughly 4% of GDP per capita for Finland, about 12-13% for Denmark and Sweden, and close to 17% for Iceland and Norway (mainland). Such losses would see GDP per capita return to levels last seen in the late-1990s or early-2000s across all five of the Nordic countries.

3.1.1. Most gains have come through increases in employment among women of parenting-age, but older female workers have contributed too

Employment outcomes and the speed and extent of progress are likely to differ across different groups of women. Unfortunately, for the Nordic countries as for many others, long time-series with information on many of the socio-demographic characteristics of employed women (like education, parenthood status, and migrant background) are not available, which prevents the construction of a detailed picture on where exactly progress has (and has not) been made. However, one area with reasonably detailed information over a relatively long period is age and the age-distribution of those in paid work.

Figure 3.3 decomposes growth in the working-age (15-64) female employment rate into parts that can be accounted for by young women aged 15-24, by parenting-age women aged 25-54, and by slightly older women aged 55-64. Again, differences in the time periods covered complicate comparisons, both across countries and also with other series, like the employment rate trends shown in Figure 3.1.[5]

For the most part, increases in female employment in the Nordic countries have been driven largely by women of parenting-age (25-54). This is no surprise given it is the widest and largest age-group covered, but nevertheless underlines the value of providing supports to women with dependent children. In Norway and Sweden, employment gains among women aged 25-54 account for about 75-80% of all increases among working-age women since the mid-1960s or early-1970s (Figure 3.3). The contributions of parenting-age women are slightly smaller in Finland (roughly 50% of all increases), Iceland (40%) and especially Denmark (about 20%), though in the latter two countries this may be as much to do with the shorter time periods covered (1991-2016 and 1983-2016, respectively) as anything else.

Figure 3.3. Most of the increase in female employment has been driven by women age 25-54, though in some countries slightly older women age 55-64 have made a substantial contribution too

Percentage point change in the female employment rate, 15-64 year-olds, and contribution by age group, longest available series, Nordic and selected other OECD member countries

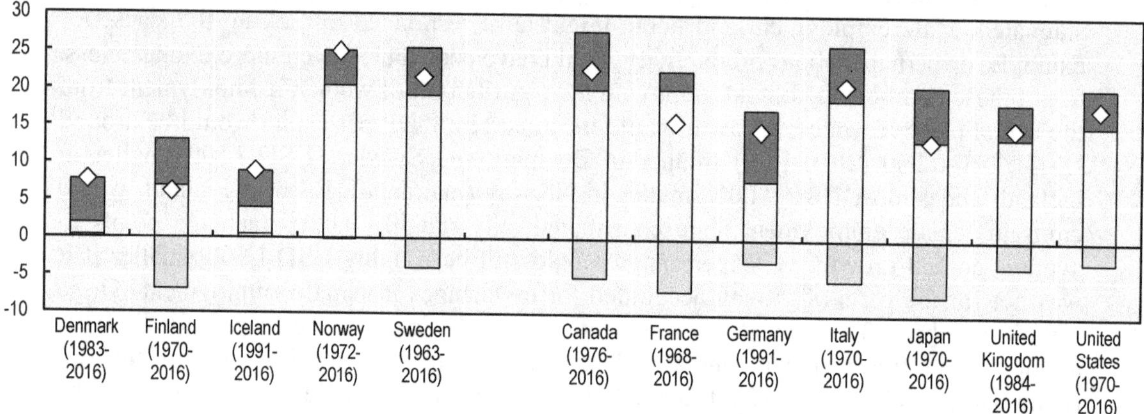

Note: Differences in the time periods covered mean estimates are not fully comparable across countries. See Annex B for more detail.

Source: *OECD* *Employment* *Database* (http://www.oecd.org/employment/emp/onlineoecdemploymentdatabase.htm).

Older female workers have also played their part (Figure 3.3). In Norway and Sweden, increases in employment among women aged 55-64 account for roughly 20-25% of all positive growth in the working-age female employment rate. In Finland and Iceland this rises to around 50%, while in Denmark it is as high as 75% (Figure 3.3) – a hugely disproportionate contribution, given that even by 2016 Danish women aged 55-64 made up less than 20% of the working-age female population. These large contributions reflect consistent increases in employment rates among women aged 55-64 – themselves largely the result of a cohort effect, with rates rising as progressively-better-educated women age

(OECD, 2017[90]). They also, however, reflect the gradual ageing of the working-age population, with slightly older women making up a much larger part of the working-age population today than four or five decades ago (*OECD Employment Database*).

Young women have generally contributed less to the overall increase (Figure 3.3). Finland and Sweden have actually seen employment decline among women aged 15-24. This isn't unusual in the OECD – many other OECD countries, including France, Italy and Japan, have also seen large decreases in the number of employed young women over the past few decades (Figure 3.3) – but does differ from Denmark, Iceland and Norway, where the number of employed women aged 15-24 has remained fairly stable (see OECD (2016[34]) and OECD (2018[35]) for more on young people in the Nordic countries).

These differences across age groups in employment gains translate in turn into differences in estimated contributions to economic growth. Simplifying slightly, and assuming for current purposes that all workers are equally productive regardless of age and other characteristics, the fact that parenting-age women (25-54) have generally contributed most to female employment growth means they also account for the bulk of women's contribution to economic growth. This is especially the case in Norway and Sweden, with changes in employment among parenting-age women are estimated to have contributed about 0.34 and 0.23 percentage points to average annual GDP per capita growth, respectively (Table A A.4 in Annex A). In Finland, Iceland, and especially Denmark, slightly older women (55-64) play a more important role (Table A A.4 in Annex A). Indeed, in Denmark, of the 0.14 percentage points that women's employment has contributed to annual growth since 1983, 0.12 percentage points can be attributed to employment gains by women aged 55-64.

3.2. Changes in employed women's working hours have made a muted contribution to economic growth in the Nordic countries

Total labour input depends not just on how many people are in paid work, but also how long they work, too. Usual working hours differ considerably in the OECD, not only within countries between men and women, for instance, but also across countries as well. For example, in countries like Greece, Korea, Mexico and Turkey, average usual weekly working hours come to well over 40 hours per week. This is 5 or so hours longer than the average in countries like Australia, Germany, and Switzerland, and more than 10 hours longer than in the Netherlands (*OECD Employment Database*). These differences add up, and can have a huge impact on an economy's total labour input. Greece, for example, currently has one of the lowest employment rates in the OECD. However, the lengthy days worked by those in employment mean the Greeks actually work more hours per person per year (770 hours per head) than some countries with far higher employment rates, like Germany (720 hours per head each year) or the Netherlands (750 hours per head each year) (*OECD National Accounts Database; OECD Employment Database*).

Women tend to be in paid work for fewer hours than men. Across the OECD as a whole, employed women are well over twice as likely as employed men to be in part-time work and, even when looking just at full-time workers, women's hours tend to be shorter than men's (*OECD Employment Database*). Overall, across the OECD, women's average usual weekly hours (34 hours per week) are about six-and-a-half hours shorter than men's average usual hours (40.5 hours per week). This pattern holds in all OECD countries, though the size of the gap differs. In Latvia, for example, the gender working hours gap is just one-and-a-half hours per week. In the Netherlands and Switzerland, it is more than ten (*OECD Employment Database*).

Gender differences in working hours are comparatively small in the Nordic countries, though to some extent this has more to do with men's relatively short working hours than women's hours (*OECD Employment Database*). In Denmark, Finland, Norway and Sweden, men work for an average of somewhere between 35 and 39 hours per week – the shortest average male hours in the OECD, with the exception of the Netherlands – and women an average of around 31-32 (Denmark and Norway) or 35 (Finland and Sweden) hours per week – close to the average for the OECD (34 hours per week in 2016; *OECD Employment Database*). Sweden has the smallest gender gap of the five Nordic OECD countries (at just over three-and-a-half hours per week), followed by Denmark, Finland, and then Norway (all at between four and five hours per week).

Iceland is different. Average usual working hours for women in Iceland are around 35 hours per week, but men's hours are much longer. In 2016, employed men in Iceland worked for an average of more than 43 hours per week (*OECD Employment Database*). Different factors are thought to have contributed to the relatively long working hours among men in Iceland. Back in the 1970s, national income levels were about two-thirds of what they were in Denmark, Norway and Sweden (Figure A A.3 in Annex A), and with a relatively small welfare state (Figure 2.3) and lower wages than in other Nordic countries, participation rates (also beyond age 65) and working hours among men in Iceland have traditionally been comparatively high (Ólafsdóttir and Ólafsson, 2014[91]). However, since the Great Recession average male working hours in Iceland fell from 47 hours per week in 2007 to 43 hours per week in 2010. They have not rebounded since, so there is some convergence in working hours among men in Nordic countries.

In the Nordic countries, as also in much of the OECD, gender differences in working hours have fallen slightly in recent decades. Men's average usual working hours have been declining for decades – among the Nordic OECD members, the steepest drop has been in Iceland (down more than six hours since the early-1990s, from an estimated 49.7 hours per week in 1991 to 43.3 in 2016), but Denmark, Finland and Norway have also seen large declines too (Figure A A.2. in Annex A). At the same time, women's average working hours have remained more or less stable (Figure 3.4). The share of employed women in part-time work has actually fallen over the past couple of decades in all of the Nordic countries except Finland (*OECD Employment Database*), but shifts elsewhere – including declines in average hours *among* part-time and, in Denmark and Iceland, also full-time female workers (*OECD Employment Database*) – have led to the overall average remaining steady. In Denmark, for example, women's average weekly hours fluctuated around 31-32 hours per week throughout the 1980s and 1990s and, although they fell slightly in recent years, are still only an hour and a half shorter now than in 1983. Even in Finland, which has seen the largest change of the five Nordic OECD members, women's average hours have fallen only by a little over two hours since 1990 (Figure 3.4).

The general 'flatness' of the trend in women's average working hours means they have not contributed a huge amount to economic growth in recent decades. Figure 3.5 summarises results from a second growth accounting exercise, with growth in GDP per capita broken down into parts that can be accounted for, as before, by growth in labour productivity, by the working-age share of the population, and by male and female headcount employment, but also this time by changes in male and female average working hours too. It should be pointed out that, because time-series on working hours are typically shorter than those on headcount employment, the period covered by this exercise is shorter than the period covered in Figure 3.2. This means that the overall average growth rate and estimates for the contributions of the various factors may differ slightly from those discussed earlier.

By and large, changes in women's working hours seem to have made little (if any) contribution to economic growth in the Nordic countries over the years covered by Figure 3.5. Of the five Nordic OECD members, Iceland and Norway have seen the largest estimated contributions to average annual growth from women's working hours, at roughly 0.15 percentage points each. This corresponds to around 8-9% of the total overall average annual growth rate in both countries. In Denmark and Sweden, changes in women's hours worked have contributed less than 0.05 percentage points to the average annual rate of growth, while in Finland they have made a small negative contribution (-0.09 percentage points).

It is important that these comparatively small contributions are considered in context. First, the overall trend is actually for declining average working hours, and changes in men's hours have contributed negatively to recent economic growth in all of the Nordic OECD members bar Sweden, sometimes by as much as around half a percentage point (Iceland) or more (Norway) (Figure 3.5). From this perspective, although women's hours might not have made much *positive* contribution to economic growth in recent years, they at least do not represent a historic drag on growth in the same way as men's hours. Second, because for data reasons the time period covered by Figure 3.5 is limited mostly to the mid-to-late-1980s onwards, these estimates take no account of any progress made on women's hours during the 1960s and 1970s, or indeed during earlier decades. It is possible that women's hours made more substantial contributions to growth in earlier years, for instance, but that such contributions are not being picked up here. Put differently, it is still possible that changes in women's working hours have contributed to past growth in the Nordic countries, though unfortunately there is little evidence of it here.

Figure 3.4. Women's average working hours have remained largely stable in the Nordic countries, and declined slightly in some other countries

Female average usual weekly working hours, all ages, 1975-2016, selected OECD countries

Panel A. Nordic OECD member countries

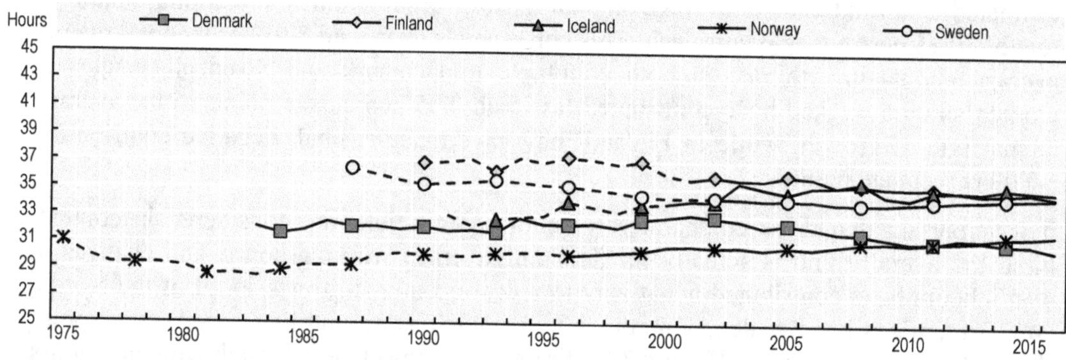

Panel B. Selected other OECD member countries

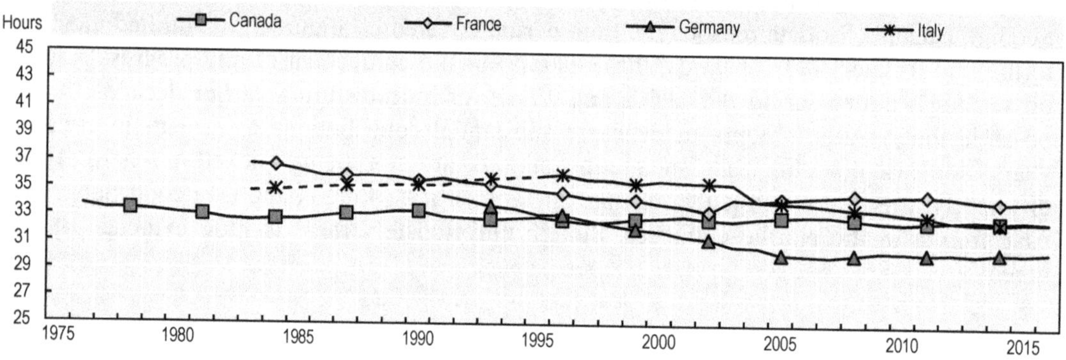

Panel C. Selected other OECD member countries (cont.)

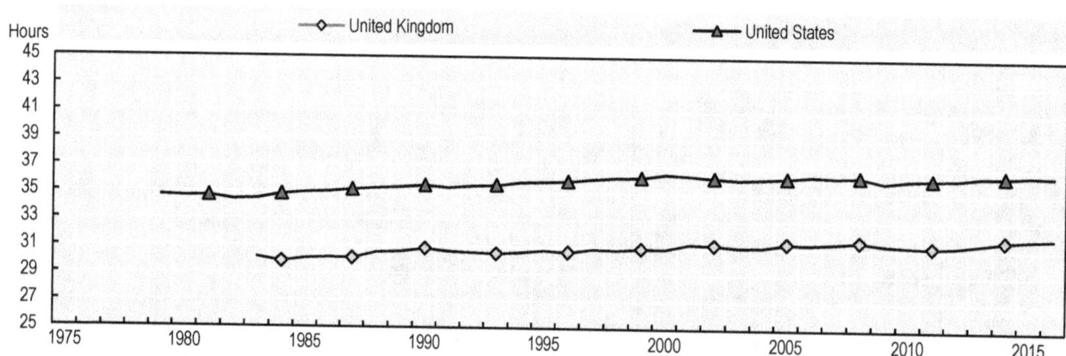

Note: Data refer to average usual weekly working hours in the main job, and cover all employed (both employees and self-employed) of all ages. Data for the United States refer to dependent employees, only. Dashed lines reflect estimated data points (see Annex B).

Source: *OECD Employment Database* (http://www.oecd.org/employment/emp/onlineoecdemploymentdatabase.htm), and OECD estimates based on data from the *OECD Annual Labour Force Statistics Database* (http://stats.oecd.org/index.aspx?queryid=451), Eurostat (http://ec.europa.eu/eurostat/data/database), and national statistical offices (see Annex B).

Figure 3.5. Changes in women's working hours have generally made little contribution to economic growth

Average annual rate of growth in GDP per capita and disaggregation of growth into its primary components, longest available series, Nordic and selected other OECD member countries

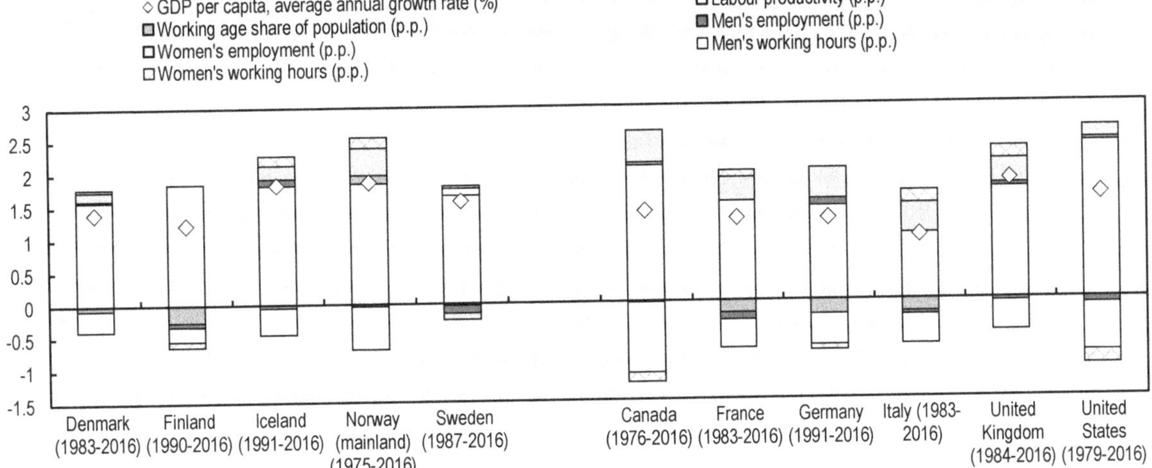

Note: Estimates based on the decomposition of national accounts data using labour force survey estimates. Differences in the time periods covered mean estimates are not fully comparable across countries. See Annex B for details.

Source: OECD estimates based on data from the *OECD National Accounts Database* (http://www.oecd.org/std/na/), the *OECD Employment Database* (http://www.oecd.org/employment/emp/onlineoecdemploymentdatabase.htm), the European Commission's *AMECO Database* (http://ec.europa.eu/economy_finance/ameco/user/serie/SelectSerie.cfm), *Eurostat* (http://ec.europa.eu/eurostat/data/database), and national statistical offices (see Annex B).

3.3. The Nordics' gender-equal employment outcomes continue to contribute to their relative prosperity

The economic gains from promoting women's employment are not a one-time thing. A lasting increase in labour input contributes to economic output on a continual basis so, as long as gains is retained, boosting female employment and improving women's economic opportunities should continue to pay dividends year after year. The Nordic countries have maintained their exceptionally high levels of female employment for decades now – indeed, as discussed earlier, even though almost all OECD countries have made progress on gender in recent years (OECD, 2017[21]) the Nordics continue to boast some of the smallest gender employment and working hours gaps in the OECD (see Table 1.1, for example). They are also, to differing extents, relatively prosperous countries with comparatively high levels of GDP per capita. This raises questions, then, around how much the Nordics continue to gain even today from their comparatively high levels of female employment; how much of their current relative prosperity can be accounted for by their relatively gender-equal labour markets, for example, or how much is the maintenance of their top-performer status on gender worth in terms of current economic output?

Figure 3.6 summarises results from what is known as a development accounting analysis – an exercise similar to growth accounting, but focused on differences in economic output *across* economies at a single point in time rather than within a single economy over time (see Annex B). In this case, GDP per capita in each of the Nordic countries (plus selected other OECD members) is compared to the OECD-30 total – an aggregate stretching across all OECD countries except for Chile, Iceland, Japan, Mexico, and Turkey, who are excluded for data reasons – with any differences or 'gaps' in GDP per capita then decomposed into their constituent parts. Denmark, Iceland, Norway (mainland) and Sweden all have positive GDP per capita gaps – each have levels of GDP per capita higher than the OECD-30 total, by about USD 8 000 (2010 PPP) (Norway), USD 2 400 (2010 PPP) (Denmark), USD 2 200 (2010 PPP) (Sweden) and USD 140 (2010 PPP) (Iceland). Finland's GDP per capita is slightly lower than the OECD-30 total (by about USD 4 000 (2010 PPP)). Similar to the earlier growth accounting analyses, these gaps are decomposed into parts that can be accounted for by differences in labour productivity, by differences in the working-age share of the population, by differences in male and female headcount employment, and by differences in male and female working hours. Values are expressed in 2010 U.S. Dollars at purchasing power parity (USD 2010 PPP).

Figure 3.6 suggests that gender equality contributes a considerable amount to the current relative prosperity of the Nordic countries. Female employment is generally not *the* most important driver of the gaps in GDP per capita: in both Denmark and Norway (mainland), for example, above-average labour productivity accounts for the bulk of their above-average GDP per capita, while in Iceland long working hours are more important (Figure 3.6). Nevertheless, across the five Nordic OECD members, women's comparatively favourable employment outcomes continue to make a positive contribute to their relative GDP per capita.

The Nordic countries' comparatively high levels of female employment are particularly important. Relative to the levels seen across the OECD-30 as a whole, the Nordics' higher-than-average female employment rates account for roughly USD 2 000-2 500 (2010 PPP) of the GDP per capita gap in Denmark, Norway and Sweden, and almost USD 5 000 (2010 PPP) in Iceland (Figure 3.6). Even in Finland, where the GDP per capita gap is negative, female employment makes a positive contribution of just under USD 1 000 (2010 PPP). Again, as with the growth accounting estimates discussed earlier, it is difficult to predict what the Nordic economies would look like *without* their current high levels of female employment – in those fictitious economies, the remaining female workers might work much longer hours, for instance. The loose suggestion, though, is that if female employment rates were typical for the OECD and equal only to those seen across the OECD-30 as whole then, depending on the country, annual GDP per capita might be somewhere between USD 1 000 and 5 000 2010 PPP smaller than it actually is today.

Figure 3.6. The Nordic countries' higher-than-average levels of female employment contribute substantially to national income, but the contribution of working hours is mixed

Gap in GDP per capita relative to the OECD-30 total and decomposition of the gap into its primary components, USD 2010 PPP, 2015, Nordic and selected other OECD member countries

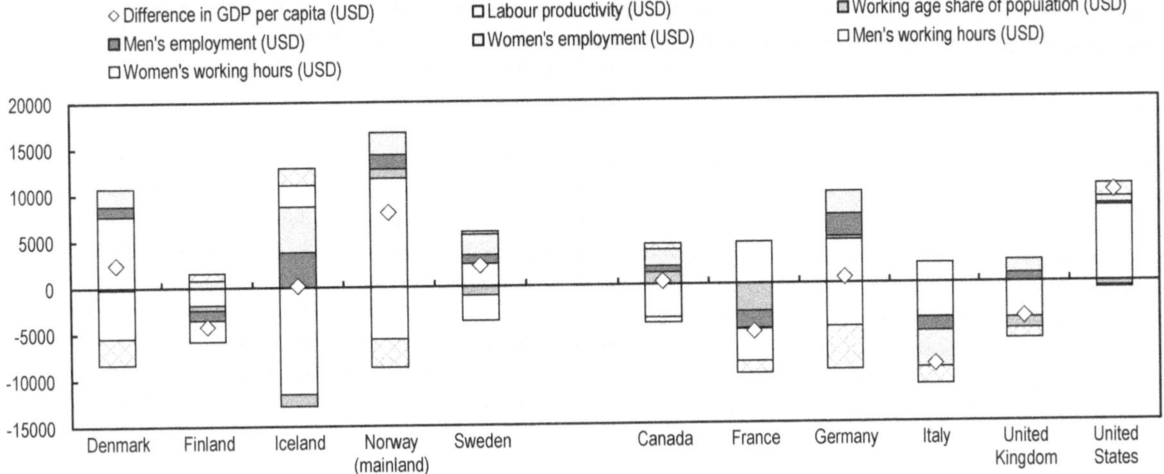

Note: Estimates based on the decomposition of national accounts data using labour force survey estimates. Differences in definitions and the data used mean estimates are not fully comparable across countries. The OECD-30 total is the weighted total across 30 OECD countries, with Chile, Iceland, Japan, Mexico and Turkey the five countries not included. See Annex B for more details.
Source: OECD estimates based on data from the *OECD National Accounts Database* (http://www.oecd.org/std/na/), the *OECD Employment Database* (http://www.oecd.org/employment/emp/onlineoecdemploymentdatabase.htm), the European Commission's *AMECO Database* (http://ec.europa.eu/economy_finance/ameco/user/serie/SelectSerie.cfm), Eurostat (http://ec.europa.eu/eurostat/data/database), and national statistical offices (see Annex B).

Working hours make less of a contribution to current relative levels of GDP per capita. In Iceland, women's relatively high working hours account for roughly USD 1 800 (2010 PPP) of the gap in GDP per capita with the OECD-30, while in Finland this is about USD 800 (2010 PPP) and in Sweden roughly USD 300 (2010 PPP). However, in Denmark and Norway, women's lower-than-average working hours might actually make a negative contribution to current GDP per capita, in both cases of around USD 3 000 (2010 PPP). Causal claims are tricky here, and it is difficult to know what would happen if women would increase their hours in paid work. For example, labour productivity is currently much higher in Norway and Denmark than it is across the OECD-30 as a whole, and pushing workers to put in longer hours might see productivity fall. Nevertheless, in these two countries in particular, women's comparatively short working hours represent one area where it is *possible* that further economic gains could be made.

4. Not there yet: Potential for further gains in the Nordic countries

So where do the Nordics go from here? Despite the long-term narrowing of gender employment gaps in the Nordic countries and the progress made in promoting women's economic opportunities, persistent gender gaps remain. These gaps are usually small, at least in comparison to other OECD countries. For example, in the Nordics as in all other OECD countries, women are still less likely to be in paid work than men (see Section 2 and Section 3.1). They are also likely to work shorter hours than men (see Section 3.2) and to work in different occupations or sectors of the economy, and all too often still struggle to progress in their careers (OECD, 2017[21]). There are still further gains to be made from narrowing gender gaps in the labour market.

This section looks forward, and aims to measure how much the Nordic countries could gain from closing remaining gender gaps in employment outcomes. It concentrates first on the potential economic gains from closing the Nordics' remaining (and comparatively small) gender gaps in headcount labour participation (Section 4.1). This exercise includes the potential benefits to the Nordic countries of meeting the G20's "25% by 2025" target – a benchmark target for international progress on gender equality in labour participation established by the G20 in 2014 (OECD et al., 2014[20]) – but also goes further to explore the possible gains from fully closing the gender participation gap (see Section 4.1). It then shifts focus to the potential (and much larger) benefits of closing gender gaps in working hours as well (Section 4.2). This latter goal is admittedly ambitious; as discussed in Section 3.3, even in the Nordic countries, women's average working hours have barely changed in the past few decades. The Nordic countries seem best placed to be setting ambitious targets and achieving gender equality.

The results shown in this section are based on estimates drawn from a combination of the OECD's in-house labour force projection models and a modified version of the OECD's long-term growth models (as presented in OECD (2014[92]), *OECD Economic Outlook No. 95*; see Annex B and Johansson et al. (2013[89]) for details). They take the OECD's standard baseline projections for both the size of the labour force and economic output and adjust estimates based on a given set of assumptions about changes in gender gaps in labour participation and, later, also working hours. The projection period used runs until 2040 – a moderate period that stretches far enough into the future to allow for major changes in gender gaps to be feasible, at least.

As with the growth accounting results shown in the previous section, these estimates have limits that should be pointed out here at the outset. For example, it should be noted that these estimates are mechanical estimates only, and assume that any changes in labour participation rates or working hours do not interact with or have any indirect effects on any other inputs (like physical or human capital). They also take no account of the possible effects of changes in paid work on unpaid work within the home, and assume that worker productivity is identical across all workers regardless of characteristics. Given that young women are as well-educated (if not more) as young men, their increased contributions to the labour market may go well beyond the pure counting of hours worked. Lastly, it is also worth pointing out that, for technical reasons, the measures and units used here differ slightly from those used in Section 3 – while those earlier results concentrated on employment rates and a 15-64 year-old age group, the estimates here are based on labour force participation rates (i.e. the employed plus unemployed population) and a 15-74 year-old age group. This is to help ensure compatibility with the inputs used for the OECD's standard long-term growth models (see Annex B, Johansson et al. (2013[89]) and OECD (2014[92])) and because the participation of over-65 workers is likely only to increase in importance in future decades.

4.1. Closing remaining gender participation gaps will produce only relatively small economic benefits for the Nordic countries

Both men and women in the Nordic countries have comparatively high and almost equal labour force participation rates. For the most part, closing the remaining (comparatively small) gender gaps in labour participation will have only a small effect on labour input and economic growth in the Nordic countries – or at least, only a small effect in comparison to the potential effects in some other OECD countries, where gender gaps are often wider. To explore the possible gains from closing gender gaps in the Nordic countries, this sub-section draws up three hypothetical future scenarios, each based on a different possible future direction for the gender gap in labour force participation:

- The *baseline* scenario, where labour force participation rates of men and women (15-74) are estimated using the OECD's standard dynamic age-cohort model, which projects participation rates (by gender and five-year age groups) based on current (2007-16) rates of labour market entry and exit. This scenario services as our reference or business-as-usual scenario.
- *Scenario A: gender participation gaps reduced by 25% by 2025 and by 50% in 2040.* In this scenario, male participation rates are held at the baseline and female participation rates are projected so that the gender participation gap observed in 2012 within each five-year age group falls by 25% by 2025, and 50% by 2040. This scenario incorporates the G20 "25% by 2025" target.
- *Scenario B: gender participation gaps reduced by 50% by 2025 and 100% by 2040.* In this scenario, male participation rates are held at the baseline and female rates are projected so that the gender participation gap observed in 2012 within each five-year age group falls by 50% by 2025, and 100% (i.e. is fully closed) by 2040.

Figure 4.1 shows how the relative size of the labour force is expected to evolve in the Nordic and selected other OECD countries under each of these scenarios. It shows the labour-force-participation-to-total-population rate across the period between 2012 (the beginning of a projection period) and 2040 (the end year), under each scenario. The labour-force-participation-to-total-population rate is used here instead of the conventional labour force participation rate (among, say, just 15-64 year-olds) because to a large extent what matters for national economic performance is not just the share of the working-age population that are active in the labour market, but more the share of the overall population.

Figure 4.1. Closing remaining gender participation gaps will have only a limited impact on labour force size in the Nordics

Actual (2000-16) and projected (2017-40) labour-force-participation-to-total-population rate under different gender gap scenarios, 15-74 year-olds, 2000-40, Nordic and selected other OECD member countries, %

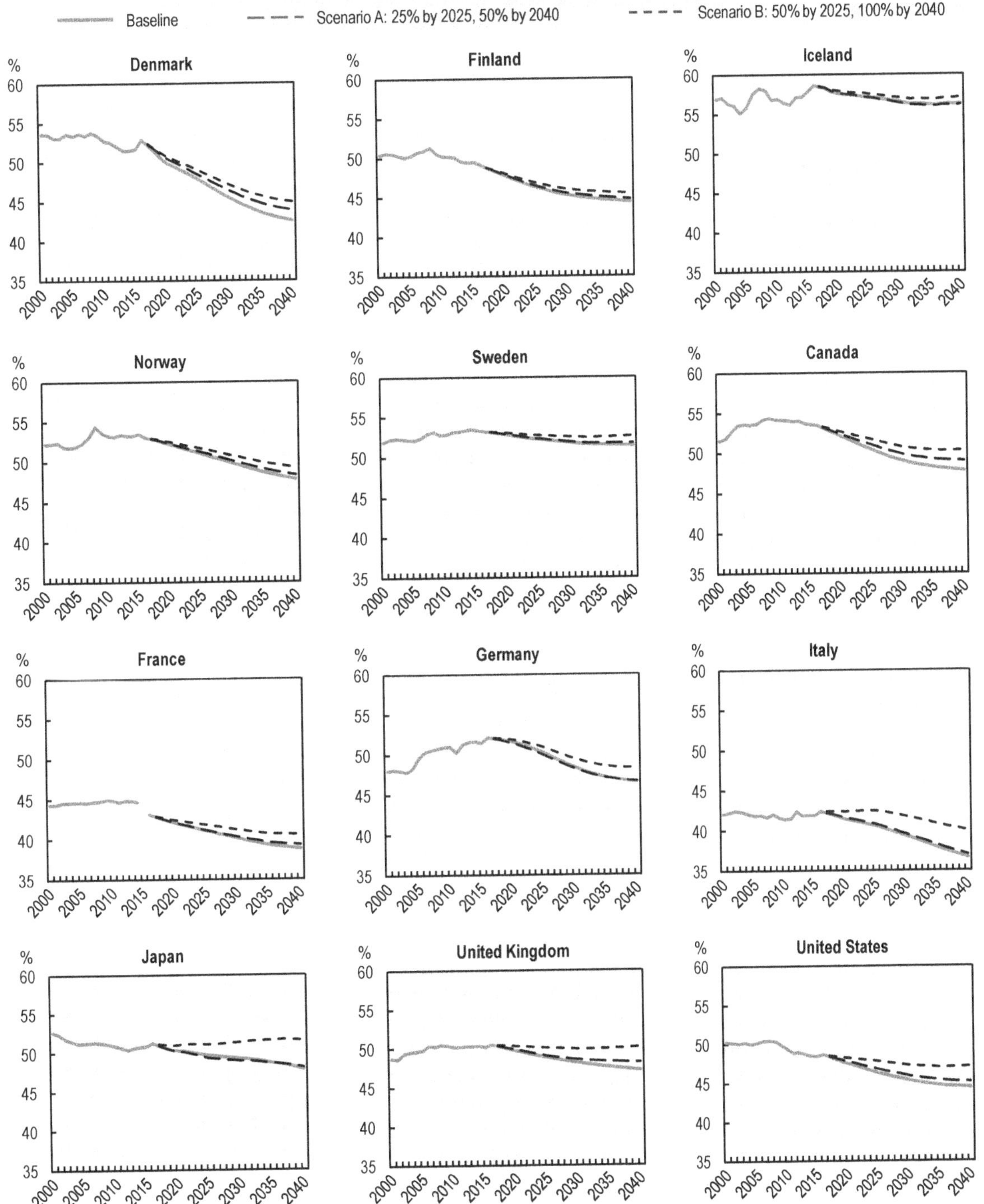

Note: See Annex B for a description of the method and data used. For France, break in series between 2014 and 2015.
Source: OECD estimates based on OECD population data and the *OECD Employment Database* (http://www.oecd.org/employment/emp/onlineoecdemploymentdatabase.htm).

In many countries, the share of the population active in the labour market is expected to fall over the next few decades. Under the baseline estimates shown in Figure 4.1 – which serve here as our reference or business-as-usual scenario – the labour-force-participation-to-total-population rate is projected to decline at least slightly in all of the Nordic and selected other OECD countries bar Iceland, and in most, it is set to decline by at least four or five percentage points (Figure 4.1). Among the Nordic countries, the largest projected decreases are in Finland and Norway, where the labour-force-participation-to-total-population rate is projected to decline by about six percentage points between 2012 and 2040, and in Denmark (almost ten percentage points).

Ageing populations and a decline in the working-age share of the population explain at least a part of these projected decreases – fewer people of working-age mean that even if labour participation rates remain constant, a smaller share of the overall population will be active in the labour market. Denmark and Finland are currently set to be hit hardest by population ageing, as the effects of historically comparatively low fertility rates feed their way through (*OECD Family Database*). However, in some cases recent trends in labour participation also play a role, especially recent trends among young people. In Finland, Norway and especially Denmark, labour force participation rates for young people (15-24 year-olds) and adults in their late-20s (25-29 year-olds) have fallen in recent years, partly because they are staying longer in education but also because of increases in the number not in employment, education or training (NEET) (*OECD Education Database*). While it is impossible to predict exactly how these young people will behave in later life, the labour force projection model used here expects at least a certain number will stay outside the labour force over the longer term, leading to decreases in overall participation rates as these cohorts age.

Closing gender participation gaps and boosting female participation can help offset these expected labour force declines (Figure 4.1). Almost all of the countries shown in Figure 4.1 see the expected decline decrease when gender gaps are closed – especially under Scenario B, where the gap is assumed to be closed fully by 2040 – but the size of the effect varies.

Looking in more detail at the Nordic countries, the estimates shown in Figure 4.1 suggest the Danish labour force would benefit most from closing remaining gender participation gaps. There, halving the gender participation gap (scenario A) would reduce the projected decline in the labour-force-participation-to-total-population rate by 1.3 percentage points, while closing it fully (scenario B) would reduce the decline by about 2.4 percentage points. This is partly because the current actual gender participation gap is slightly larger in Denmark than in the other Nordic countries (see Table 1.1), but also because closing the gender gap helps avoid a comparatively steep projected decline in female participation in Denmark. The effects are smaller in the remaining four Nordic countries; in all four, even fully closing the gender gap (scenario B) would provide a bump to the labour-force-participation-to-total-population rate of only around 1-1.5 percentage points. Put differently, in these countries, relative to the baseline, even completely abolishing the gender participation gap by 2040 would increase the number of workers per 100 persons by only about one or one-and-a-half.

4.1.1. A modest effect on future growth

Unsurprisingly, such small gains in projected labour input are expected to have only a fairly limited impact on projected future GDP per capita and GDP per capita growth. Figure 4.2 shows estimates of the effects of closing the gender participation gaps on the average annual rate of growth in GDP per capita over the period 2013-40. For the Nordic countries, closing the gender participation gap by half by 2040 (scenario A) is estimated to increase projected annual GDP per capita growth rates by only around 0.00-0.07 percentage points, while even fully closing the gap by 2040 (scenario B) is estimated to provide a boost of roughly only 0.05-0.10 percentage points. The largest potential gains are in Denmark, where fully closing the gender gap (scenario B) could boost average annual growth by about 0.13 percentage points. This is equivalent to a 5.5 percentage point boost in cumulative GDP per capita growth over the 2013-40 period as a whole, and would be worth about USD 1 700 2005 PPP in additional GDP per capita by 2040. However, even this potential gain pales in comparison to those on offer in countries with larger participation gaps like Italy and Japan (0.19 percentage points and 0.18 percentage points under scenario B; see Figure 4.2), and especially in some of the younger OECD countries with very low female participation rates such as Mexico and Turkey (0.52 and 0.42 percentage points under scenario B; see Table A A.7 in Annex A).

Figure 4.2. Further gains in growth from closing gender participation gaps in Nordic countries are relatively modest

Estimated difference relative to the baseline in the projected average annual rate of growth in GDP per capita over the period 2013-2040, different gender gap scenarios (closing gender gaps in labour force participation only), percentage points, Nordic and selected other OECD member countries

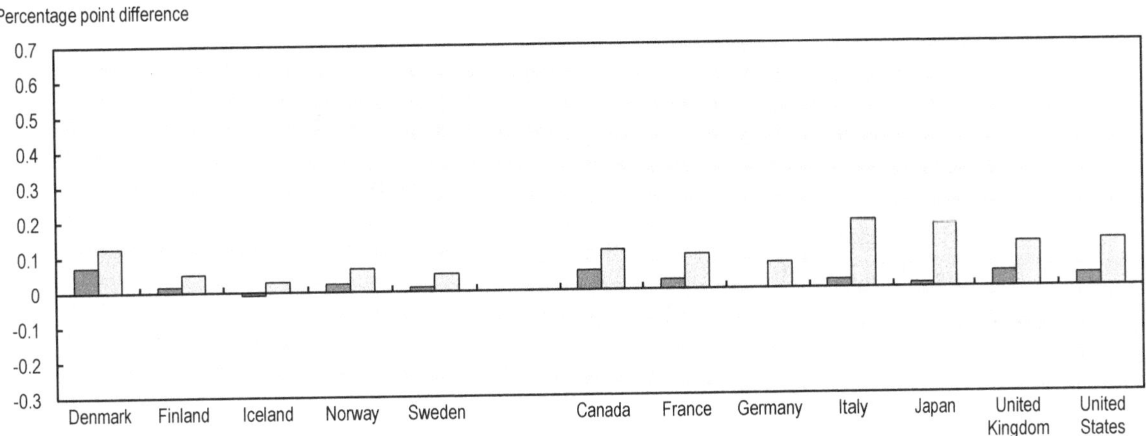

Note: LFP stands for labour force participation. See Annex B for a description of the method and data used.
Source: OECD estimates based on OECD (2014), *OECD Economic Outlook No. 95 Volume 2014 Issue 1,* OECD Publishing, Paris (http://dx.doi.org/10.1787/eco_outlook-v2014-1-en), *OECD Economic Outlook: Statistics and Projections Databases* (http://stats.oecd.org/index.aspx?dataSetCode=EO), OECD population data and the *OECD Employment Database* (http://www.oecd.org/employment/emp/onlineoecdemploymentdatabase.htm).

4.2. Closing remaining gender working hours gaps could extend economic gains in the Nordic countries

Trying to close headcount participation gaps is one thing, achieving greater gender equality in working hours is quite another. As discussed earlier in Section 3.2, gender gaps in workings hours are comparatively small but have proven sticky. While men's working hours have fallen slightly in recent decades, women's have barely changed. This is one area where the Nordics could extract further sizeable economic gains; boosting labour input by closing gender working hours gaps and increasing women's working hours would carry considerable economic benefits for the Nordic countries.

To illustrate the potential gains from closing gender gaps in working hours in addition to gender gaps in labour participation, this section draws on the following hypothetical scenarios:

- The *baseline* scenario, with labour force participation rates for men and women (15-74) estimated using the OECD's standard dynamic age-cohort model, which projects participation rates (by gender and five-year age groups) based on current (2007-16) rates of labour market entry and exit. In addition, average usual weekly working hours for each gender and five year age group are held constant at their 2016 values.
- *Scenario C: gender participation gaps and gender working hours gaps reduced by 25% by 2025 and by 50% by 2040, with women increasing working hours.* This scenario assumes that gender gaps in both labour force participation rates and usual weekly working hours decline for each five year age group by 25% by 2025 and 50% by 2040, with the gender working hours gap closed entirely through increases in *female* working hours (male hours follow the baseline).
- *Scenario D: gender participation gaps and gender working hours gaps reduced by 25% by 2025 and by 50% by 2040, with men decreasing working hours.* This scenario is the same as scenario C, but gender working hours gap closed entirely through decreases in male hours, rather than increases in female hours. Female hours follow the baseline.
- *Scenario E: gender participation gaps and gender working hours gaps reduced by 50% by 2025 and by 100% by 2040, with women increasing working hours.* This is a "full convergence" scenario. It assumes that gender gaps in both labour force participation rates and usual weekly working hours decline for each five year age group by 50% by 2025 and 100% (i.e. are fully closed) by 2040, with the gender working hours gap closed entirely through increases in *female* working hours (male hours follow the baseline).

In the Nordic countries as elsewhere, closing gender working hours gaps by increasing women's hours would lead to large increases in overall average working hours. Figure 4.3 shows the estimated impact of closing working hours gaps on projected overall average usual weekly working hours over the years to 2040. Across all the included countries, halving gender working hours gaps through *increases in women's hours* (scenario C) would boost overall average weekly working hours by at least three-quarters of an hour by 2040 – an increase of between 2 and 5% on the baseline in most of the covered countries – while closing the gap completely (scenario E) would lead to an increases of at least one hour and three-quarters by 2040 – equivalent to a boost of at least 5%. Closing the gender gap through *decreases in men's hours* (scenario D), in contrast, would of course have broadly the opposite effect. In all the countries included in Figure 4.3, closing the gap even by just half through a decrease in men's average hours would see the overall average drop by around an hour per week or more by 2040.

Figure 4.3. Closing gender working hours gaps by increasing women's hours could lead to large increases in overall hours worked

Actual (2000-16) and projected (2017-40) average usual weekly working hours under different gender gap scenarios, 15-74 year-olds, 2000-40, Nordic and selected other OECD member countries, %

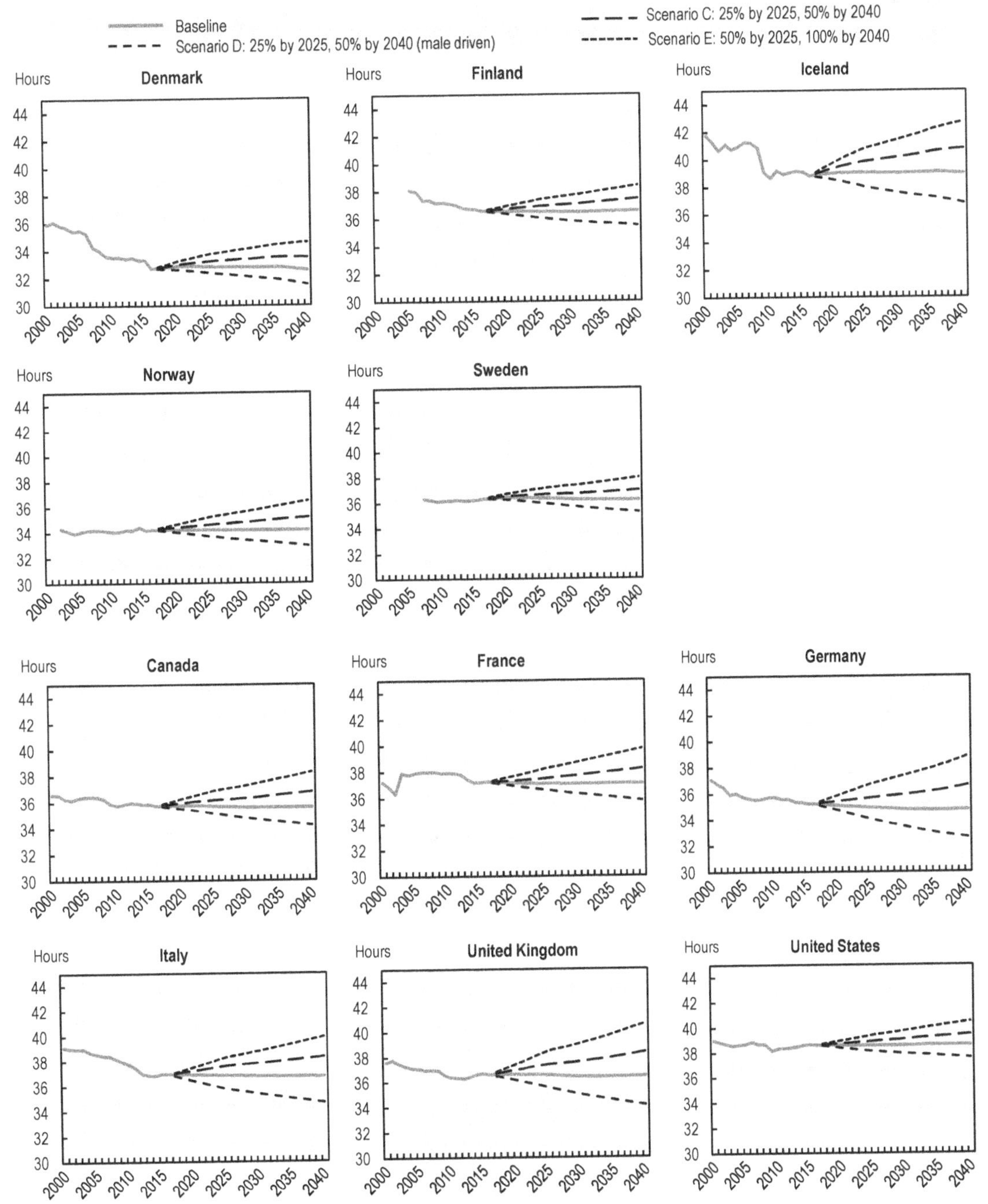

Note: See Annex B for a description of the method and data used.
Source: OECD estimates based on OECD population data and the *OECD Employment Database* (http://www.oecd.org/employment/emp/onlineoecdemploymentdatabase.htm).

Of the five Nordic countries, potential gains from closing the gender working hours gap are largest in Iceland (Figure 4.3). Because of the comparatively large existing hours gap in Iceland (see Section 3.2), closing the gap fully through increases in women's hours (scenario E) could lead to an increase in overall average hours of as much as almost four hours per week by 2040. However, the remaining four Nordic countries could also see large gains. In all four, fully closing the gap would boost average weekly hours by between one-and-three-quarters and two-and-a-quarter hours – in all cases equivalent to a boost in overall hours of around 5-7%.

Of course, whether or not it is feasible or even desirable to fully close gender hours gaps through only increases in women's hours is open to discussion. In Iceland, for example, doing so would require both employed men and employed women to work an average of just less than 43 hours per week. This would severely limit time available for unpaid work inside the home, and put huge pressure on families' abilities to reconcile work and care responsibilities. On the other hand, in all Nordic countries, except Norway the share of women involuntarily working part-time is above the OECD average (OECD, 2017[41]), so there may be some scope for increases in hours. In any case, hypothetically, the potential gains in terms of raw labour input from closing gender hours gaps are large.

The potential boost to Nordic growth and GDP per capita from closing gender working hours gaps as well as gender participation gaps could be substantial. Figure 4.4 shows estimates of the impact of closing both gender participation and gender working hours gaps on projected average annual growth in GDP per capita over the period 2013-40. Across the five Nordic countries, the boost to labour input delivered by halving gender gaps in both participation and hours (scenario C) could add roughly around 0.10 percentage points to projected annual GDP per capita growth over the years 2013-40, while going further and closing both gaps fully (scenario E) could add as much as around 0.25-0.40 percentage points. This is the equivalent of boosting projected annual GDP per capita growth by roughly 15-30%, depending on the country. The largest potential gains are again in Denmark (0.42 percentage points in scenario E), thanks in large part to the greater gains derived from closing the participation gap (see Section 4.1). However, potential gains also very large in Iceland (0.39 percentage points in scenario E, due more to gains from closing the working hours gap) and Norway (0.35 percentage points in scenario E, driven by a combination of gains from closing both gaps). In terms of overall growth over the 2013-2040 period as a whole, these potential gains are equivalent to boosting cumulative GDP per capita growth by somewhere between 12 (Finland and Sweden) and 19 percentage points (Denmark). In dollar terms, they would translate by 2040 into increases in GDP per capita (relative to the baseline) of around USD 3 900 (2005 PPP) in Finland, USD 4 300 in Sweden, USD 5 600 in Iceland, USD 6 100 in Denmark and USD 8 200 in Norway.

Figure 4.4. The gains in growth from closing gender working hours gaps as well as gender participation gaps could be substantial

Estimated difference relative to the baseline in the projected average annual rate of growth in GDP per capita over the period 2013-2040, different gender gap scenarios (closing gender gaps in labour force participation and working hours), percentage points, Nordic and selected other OECD member countries

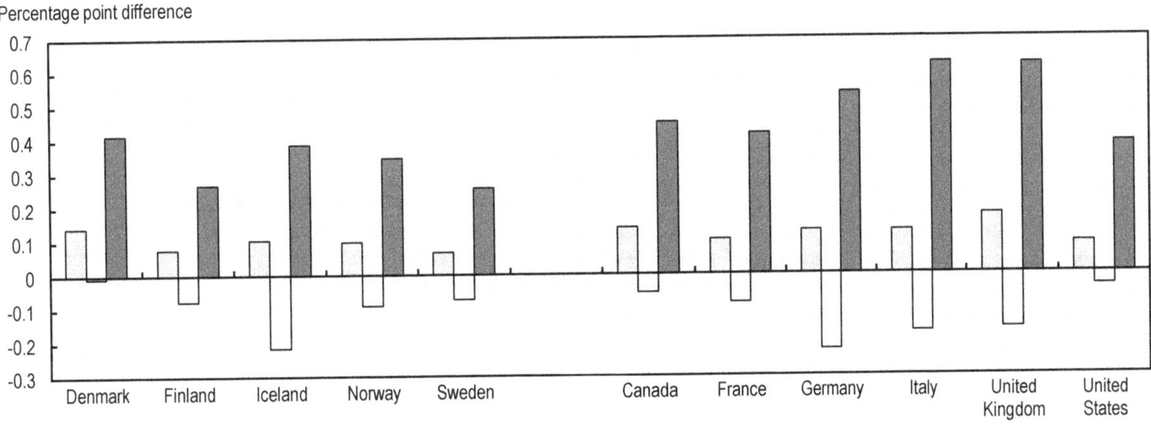

Note: LFP stands for labour force participation. See Annex B for a description of the method and data used.
Source: OECD estimates based on OECD (2014), *OECD Economic Outlook No. 95 Volume 2014 Issue 1*, OECD Publishing, Paris (http://dx.doi.org/10.1787/eco_outlook-v2014-1-en), *OECD Economic Outlook: Statistics and Projections Databases* (http://stats.oecd.org/index.aspx?dataSetCode=EO), OECD population data and the *OECD Employment Database* (http://www.oecd.org/employment/emp/onlineoecdemploymentdatabase.htm).

References

Adema, W. (2012), "Setting the scene: The mix of family policy objectives and packages across the OECD", *Children and Youth Services Review*, Vol. 34/3, http://dx.doi.org/10.1016/j.childyouth.2011.10.007. [23]

Adema, W., C. Clarke and V. Frey (2015), "Paid Parental Leave: Lessons from OECD Countries and Selected U.S. States", *OECD Social, Employment and Migration Working Papers*, No. 172, OECD Publishing, Paris, http://dx.doi.org/10.1787/5jrqgvqqb4vb-en. [77]

Adema, W., P. Fron and M. Ladaique (2014), "How much do OECD countries spend on social protection and how redistributive are their tax/benefit systems?", *International Social Security Review*, Vol. 67/1, pp. 1-25, http://dx.doi.org/10.1111/issr.12028. [62]

Adema, W., P. Fron and M. Ladaique (2011), "Is the European Welfare State Really More Expensive?: Indicators on Social Spending, 1980-2012; and a Manual to the OECD Social Expenditure Database (SOCX)", *OECD Social, Employment and Migration Working Papers*, No. 124, OECD Publishing, Paris, http://dx.doi.org/10.1787/5kg2d2d4pbf0-en. [59]

Angelov, N. and E. Lindahl (2016), "Parenthood and the Gender Gap in Pay", *Journal of Labor Economics*, Vol. 34/3, https://www.journals.uchicago.edu/doi/pdfplus/10.1086/684851 (accessed on 10 April 2018). [46]

Azevedo, J. et al. (2013), "Is Labor Income Responsible for Poverty Reduction? A Decomposition Approach", *World Bank Policy Research Working Papers*, No. 6414, http://dx.doi.org/10.1596/1813-9450-6414. [94]

Barro, R. and J. Lee (2013), "A new data set of educational attainment in the world, 1950–2010", *Journal of Development Economics*, Vol. 104, pp. 184-198, http://dx.doi.org/10.1016/J.JDEVECO.2012.10.001. [32]

Bladini, M. (2017), *Hat och hot på nätet : en kartläggning av den rättsliga regleringen i Norden från ett jämställdhetsperspektiv*, Nordic Information on Gender (NIKK) , Göteborg, http://norden.diva-portal.org/smash/record.jsf?pid=diva2%3A1117521&dswid=-3564 (accessed on 12 April 2018). [65]

Blum, S., A. Koslowski and P. Moss (2017), *International Review of Leave Policies and Related Research 2017*, International Network on Leave Policies and Research, http://www.leavenetwork.org/fileadmin/Leavenetwork/Annual_reviews/2017_Leave_Review_2017_final2.pdf (accessed on 04 April 2018). [79]

Brandth, B. et al. (2012), *Parental leave, childcare and gender equality in the Nordic countries*, Nordic Council of Ministers, Copenhagen K, http://dx.doi.org/10.6027/TN2011-562. [25]

Causa, O. and M. Hermansen (2017), "Income redistribution through taxes and transfers across OECD countries", *OECD Economics Department Working Papers*, No. 1453, OECD Publishing, Paris, http://dx.doi.org/10.1787/bc7569c6-en. [61]

Cho, S. (2016), "Does Gender Equality Promote Social Trust? An Empirical Analysis", *World Development*, Vol. 88, pp. 175-187, http://dx.doi.org/10.1016/J.WORLDDEV.2016.07.019. [10]

Cuberes, D. and M. Teignier (2015), "How Costly Are Labor Gender Gaps? Estimates for the Balkans and Turkey", *Policy Research Working Paper*, No. 7319, World Bank, https://openknowledge.worldbank.org/bitstream/handle/10986/22195/How0costly0are0e0Ba lkans0and0Turkey.pdf;sequence=1 (accessed on 19 March 2018). [18]

Danmarks Statistik (2015), *Kvinder og mænd i 100 år: fra ligeret mod ligestilling*, http://dx.doi.org/978-87-501-2176-3. [64]

Del Boca, D. (2015), "The impact of child care costs and availability on mothers' labor supply", *ImPRovE Working Papers*, No. 15/04, Herman Deleeck Centre for Social Policy, University of Antwerp, https://ideas.repec.org/p/hdl/improv/1504.html (accessed on 16 December 2017). [73]

Duval, R. and C. de la Maisonneuve (2010), "Long-run growth scenarios for the world economy", *Journal of Policy Modeling*, Vol. 32/1, pp. 64-80, http://dx.doi.org/10.1016/J.JPOLMOD.2009.10.001. [88]

EIGE (2018), *Gender Statistics Database*, European Institute for Gender Equality, http://eige.europa.eu/gender-statistics/dgs (accessed on 26 March 2018). [57]

Ellingsæter, A. (2013), "Scandinavian welfare states and gender (de) segregation: Recent trends and processes", *Economic and Industrial Democracy*, Vol. 34/3, pp. 501-518, http://dx.doi.org/10.1177/0143831X13491616. [5]

Esping-Andersen, G. (1999), *Social foundations of postindustrial economies*, Oxford University Press, https://books.google.fr/books?hl=en&lr=&id=yeXnCwAAQBAJ&oi=fnd&pg=PR7&dq=esp ing-andersen&ots=rr9FkxyuEd&sig=YSVPKQkjGsMOvfEanwPjjTfMqvE#v=onepage&q=espi ng-andersen&f=false (accessed on 03 April 2018). [27]

Esteve-Volart, B. (2004), "Gender Discrimination and Growth: Theory and Evidence from India", *LSE STICERD Research Paper*, No. DEDPS42, London School of Economics and Political Science, https://papers.ssrn.com/sol3/papers.cfm?abstract_id=1127011 (accessed on 19 March 2018). [16]

European Commission (2018), *AMECO Database*, http://ec.europa.eu/economy_finance/ameco/user/serie/SelectSerie.cfm (accessed on 20 April 2018). [102]

Eurostat (2018), *Eurostat Database*, http://ec.europa.eu/eurostat/data/database (accessed on 20 April 2018). [100]

Eydal, G. et al. (2015), "Trends in parental leave in the Nordic countries: has the forward march of gender equality halted?", *Community, Work & Family*, Eydal, G, Gíslason, I., Rostgaard, T., Brandth, B., Duvander, A-Z,. and Lammi-Taskula, J., http://dx.doi.org/10.1080/13668803.2014.1002754. [81]

Gallen, Y., R. Lesner and R. Vejlin (2017), "The Labor Market Gender Gap in Denmark: Sorting Out the Past 30 Years", *IZA DP No. 10789*, IZA, http://www.iza.org (accessed on 10 April 2018). [47]

Goldin, C. (1995), "The U-Shaped Female Labor Force Function in Economic Development and Economic History", in Schultz TP (ed.), *Investment in Women's Human Capital and* [12]

Economic Development, University of Chicago Press, https://scholar.harvard.edu/goldin/publications/u-shaped-female-labor-force-function-economic-development-and-economic-history (accessed on 19 March 2018).

Gornick, J. and J. Jacobs (1998), "Gender, the Welfare State, and Public Employment: A Comparative Study of Seven Industrialized Countries", *American Sociological Review*, Vol. 63/5, p. 688, http://dx.doi.org/10.2307/2657334. [51]

Government of Norway (2018), *Endringar i reglar for opptak til høgare utdanning*, Regjeringen.no, Press release No 25-18, https://www.regjeringen.no/no/aktuelt/25---18-endringar-i-reglar-for-opptak-til-hogare-utdanning/id2588338/ (accessed on 18 April 2018). [39]

Government Offices of Sweden (2016), *Annual report on state-owned enterprises 2016*, Swedish Government Offices, Stockholm, https://www.government.se/4a6e13/contentassets/e66654348c76492c8504413f3413e9a5/eng-vb-2016-final-2.pdf (accessed on 13 April 2018). [40]

Hansen, M. (1997), *THE SCANDINAVIAN WELFARE STATE MODEL: THE IMPACT OF THE PUBLIC SECTOR ON SEGREGATION AND GENDER EQUALITY*, Sage Publications, Ltd., http://dx.doi.org/10.2307/23746422. [50]

Hilson, M. (2007), "Scandinavia", in Gerwarth, R. (ed.), *Twisted paths: Europe 1914-1945*, Oxford University Press, Oxford. [1]

Holter, Ø. (2014), "What's in it for Men? Old Question, New Data", *Men and Masculinities*, Vol. 17/5, pp. 515-548, http://dx.doi.org/10.1177/1097184X14558237. [9]

Hsieh, C. et al. (2013), "The Allocation of Talent and U.S. Economic Growth", *NBER Working Paper*, No. 18693, National Bureau of Economic Research, Cambridge, MA, http://dx.doi.org/10.3386/w18693. [17]

ILO (2018), *ILOSTAT Database*, http://www.ilo.org/ilostat/ (accessed on 20 April 2018). [97]

Iqbal, R. and P. Todi (2015), "The Nordic Model: existence, emergence and sustainability", *Procedia Economics and Finance*, Vol. 30, pp. 336-351, http://dx.doi.org/10.1016/S2212-5671(15)01301-5. [63]

Jaumotte, F. (2003), "Female Labour Force Participation: Past Trends and Main Determinants in OECD Countries", *OECD Economics Department Working Papers*, No. 376, OECD Publishing, Paris, http://dx.doi.org/10.1787/082872464507. [71]

Johansson, Å. et al. (2013), "Long-Term Growth Scenarios", *OECD Economics Department Working Papers*, No. 1000, OECD Publishing, Paris, http://dx.doi.org/10.1787/5k4ddxpr2fmr-en. [89]

Kelley, D. et al. (2017), *Women's Entrepreneurship 2016/2017 Report Global Entrepreneurship Monitor*, https://www.babson.edu/Academics/centers/blank-center/global-research/gem/Documents/GEM%202016-2017%20Womens%20Report.pdf (accessed on 27 March 2018). [42]

Keloharju, M., S. Knüpfer and J. Tåg (2017), "What Prevents Female Executives from Reaching the Top? What Prevents Female Executives from Reaching the Top? *", *IFN Working Paper*, No. No. 1111, Research Institute of Industrial Economics, http://www.ifn.se (accessed on 19 February 2018). [49]

Klasen, S. (1999), "Does Gender Inequality Reduce Growth and Development? Evidence from Cross-Country Regressions", *Policy Research Report Working Paper*, No. 7, World Bank, [13]

Washington, DC,
https://www.tandfonline.com/doi/ref/10.1080/13545700902893106?scroll=top (accessed on
19 March 2018).

Klasen, S. and F. Lamanna (2009), "The Impact of Gender Inequality in Education and
Employment on Economic Growth: New Evidence for a Panel of Countries", *Feminist
Economics*, Vol. 15/3, pp. 91-132, http://dx.doi.org/10.1080/13545700902893106. [14]

Kleven, H., C. Landais and J. Søgaard (2018), *Children and Gender Inequality: Evidence from
Denmark*, National Bureau of Economic Research, Cambridge, MA,
http://dx.doi.org/10.3386/w24219. [48]

Kosunen, N. et al. (2017), *Regulation of Gender-Discriminatory Advertising in the Nordic
Countries*, Nordic Council of Ministers, Copenhagen, https://norden.diva-
portal.org/smash/get/diva2:1108955/FULLTEXT01.pdf (accessed on 17 April 2018). [67]

Kuhnle, S. and S. Hort (2004), "The Developmental Welfare State in Scandinavia: Lessons for
the Developing World", *Social Policy and Development Programme Paper*, No. 17, United
Nations Research Institute for Social Development,
https://www.files.ethz.ch/isn/102834/17.pdf (accessed on 03 April 2018). [24]

Lønkommissionen (2010), *LØN, KØN, UDDANNELSE OG FLEKSIBILITET*,
Lønkommissionen (Danish Wage Council),
http://www.lonkommissionen.dk/pdf/Sammenfatning_og_konklusion.pdf (accessed on
13 April 2018). [54]

Looze, M. et al. (2017), "The Happiest Kids on Earth. Gender Equality and Adolescent Life
Satisfaction in Europe and North America", *Journal of Youth and Adolescence*, pp. 1-13,
http://dx.doi.org/10.1007/s10964-017-0756-7. [7]

Mandel, H. (2011), "Rethinking the paradox: tradeoffs in work-family policy and patterns of
gender inequality", *Community, Work & Family*, Vol. 14/2, pp. 159-176,
http://dx.doi.org/10.1080/13668803.2011.571397. [52]

Medlingsinstitutet (2017), *Löneskillnaden mellan kvinnor och män 2016 Vad säger den
officiella lönestatistiken?*, Medlingsinstitutet (swededish national mediation Office),
Stockholm, http://www.mi.se (accessed on 13 April 2018). [55]

Mósesdóttir, L. et al. (2006), *Evaluating Equal Pay in the Nordic Countries*, Final report of the
project På sporet av likelön - Evaluating Equal Pay - Mælistikur á launajafnrétti. , Reykjavik,
http://starfsmenn.bifrost.is/Files/Skra_0013316.pdf (accessed on 20 February 2018). [53]

Nielsen, H., M. Simonsen and M. Verner (2004), "Does the Gap in Family-friendly Policies
Drive the Family Gap?*", *Scandinavian Journal of Economics*, Vol. 106/4, pp. 721-744,
http://dx.doi.org/10.1111/j.0347-0520.2004.00385.x. [45]

NIKK (2018), *Vad säger lagen om #metoo?*, http://www.nikk.no/wp-
content/uploads/metoo_sve_uppdaterad_180323.pdf (accessed on 12 April 2018). [66]

NIKK (forthcoming), *The Nordic Gender Effect at Work: Nordic briefs on parental leave,
childcare, flexible work arrangements, leadership and equal opportunities at work*, Nordic
Council of Ministers, Copenhagen. [69]

NOSOSCO (2018), *NOSOSCO Database*, http://nowbase.org/da/database (accessed on
20 April 2018). [110]

NOSOSCO (2017), *Social Protection in the Nordic Countries 2015/2016: Scope, Expenditure* [111] *and Financing*, Nordic Social Statistical Committee (NOSOSCO), http://norden.diva-portal.org/smash/get/diva2:1148493/FULLTEXT02.pdf (accessed on 21 February 2018).

NOSOSCO (2016), *Social Protection in the Nordic Countries 2014/2015: Scope, Expenditure and Financing*, Nordic Social Statistical Committee (NOSOSCO), https://norden.diva-portal.org/smash/get/diva2:1059435/FULLTEXT02.pdf (accessed on 26 February 2018).   [76]

OECD (2018), *Investing in Youth: Norway*, OECD Publishing, Paris, http://dx.doi.org/10.1787/9789264283671-en.   [35]

OECD (2018), *National Accounts Database*, http://www.oecd.org/sdd/na/ (accessed on 20 April 2018).   [101]

OECD (2018), *OECD Annual Labour Force Statistics Database*, http://dotstat.oecd.org/Index.aspx?DataSetCode=ALFS_EMP (accessed on 20 April 2018).   [99]

OECD (2018), *OECD Economic Outlook: Statistics and Projections*, http://dx.doi.org/10.1787/EO-DATA-EN.   [103]

OECD (2018), *OECD Education Database*, http://www.oecd.org/education/database.htm (accessed on 20 April 2018).   [115]

OECD (2018), *OECD Employment Database*, http://www.oecd.org/employment/emp/onlineoecdemploymentdatabase.htm (accessed on 20 April 2018).   [96]

OECD (2018), *OECD Family Database*, http://www.oecd.org/els/family/database.htm (accessed on 20 April 2018).   [112]

OECD (2018), *OECD Gender Data Portal*, http://www.oecd.org/gender/data/ (accessed on 20 April 2018).   [106]

OECD (2018), *OECD Income Distribution Database (IDD)*, http://www.oecd.org/social/income-distribution-database.htm (accessed on 20 April 2018).   [108]

OECD (2018), *OECD Revenue Statistics*, http://www.oecd.org/tax/revenue-statistics-comparable-tax-revenue-data.htm (accessed on 20 April 2018).   [107]

OECD (2018), *OECD Social Expenditure Database (SOCX)*, http://www.oecd.org/social/expenditure.htm (accessed on 20 April 2018).   [114]

OECD (2018), *OECD Tax and Benefit Systems*, http://www.oecd.org/social/benefits-and-wages.htm (accessed on 20 April 2018).   [109]

OECD (2018), *PISA 2015 Database*, http://www.oecd.org/pisa/data/ (accessed on 20 April 2018).   [104]

OECD (2017), *2013 OECD Recommendation of the Council on Gender Equality in Education, Employment and Entrepreneurship*, OECD Publishing, Paris, http://dx.doi.org/10.1787/9789264279391-en.   [28]

OECD (2017), *Dare to Share: Germany's Experience Promoting Equal Partnership in Families*, OECD Publishing, Paris, http://dx.doi.org/10.1787/9789264259157-en.   [3]

OECD (2017), *Education at a Glance 2017: OECD Indicators*, OECD Publishing, Paris, http://dx.doi.org/10.1787/eag-2017-en.   [75]

OECD (2017), *Entrepreneurship at a Glance 2017*, OECD Publishing, Paris, http://dx.doi.org/10.1787/entrepreneur_aag-2017-en.   [105]

OECD (2017), *Government at a Glance 2017*, OECD Publishing, Paris, http://dx.doi.org/10.1787/gov_glance-2017-en. [44]

OECD (2017), *OECD Economic Surveys: Iceland 2017*, OECD Publishing, Paris, http://dx.doi.org/10.1787/eco_surveys-isl-2017-en. [56]

OECD (2017), *OECD Economic Surveys: Sweden 2017*, OECD Publishing, Paris, http://dx.doi.org/10.1787/eco_surveys-swe-2017-en. [41]

OECD (2017), *Preventing Ageing Unequally*, OECD Publishing, Paris, http://dx.doi.org/10.1787/9789264279087-en. [90]

OECD (2017), *Revenue Statistics: 1965-2016*, OECD Publishing, Paris, http://dx.doi.org/10.1787/9789264283183-en. [58]

OECD (2017), *The Pursuit of Gender Equality: An Uphill Battle*, OECD Publishing, Paris, http://dx.doi.org/10.1787/9789264281318-en. [21]

OECD (2016), *2015 OECD Recommendation of the Council on Gender Equality in Public Life*, OECD Publishing, Paris, http://dx.doi.org/10.1787/9789264252820-en. [29]

OECD (2016), *Be Flexible! Background brief on how workplace flexibility can help European employees to balance work and family*, OECD, Paris, http://www.oecd.org/els/family/Be-Flexible-Backgrounder-Workplace-Flexibility.pdf (accessed on 21 February 2018). [43]

OECD (2016), *Investing in Youth: Sweden*, Investing in Youth, OECD Publishing, Paris, http://dx.doi.org/10.1787/9789264267701-en. [34]

OECD (2016), *OECD Economic Surveys: Finland 2016*, OECD Publishing, Paris, http://dx.doi.org/10.1787/eco_surveys-fin-2016-en. [31]

OECD (2016), *PISA 2015 Results (Volume I): Excellence and Equity in Education*, PISA, OECD Publishing, Paris, http://dx.doi.org/10.1787/9789264266490-en. [33]

OECD (2016), *Walking the tightrope: Background brief on parents' work-life balance across the stages of childhood*, http://www.oecd.org/els/family/Background-brief-parents-work-life-balance-stages-childhood.pdf (accessed on 16 December 2017). [70]

OECD (2016), *Working Together: Skills and Labour Market Integration of Immigrants and their Children in Sweden*, OECD Publishing, Paris, http://dx.doi.org/10.1787/9789264257382-en. [4]

OECD (2015), *In It Together: Why Less Inequality Benefits All*, OECD Publishing, Paris, http://dx.doi.org/10.1787/9789264235120-en. [11]

OECD (2015), *National Accounts at a Glance 2015*, OECD Publishing, Paris, http://dx.doi.org/10.1787/na_glance-2015-en. [84]

OECD (2015), *The ABC of Gender Equality in Education: Aptitude, Behaviour, Confidence*, PISA, OECD Publishing, Paris, http://dx.doi.org/10.1787/9789264229945-en. [37]

OECD (2014), *OECD Economic Outlook, Volume 2014 Issue 1*, OECD Publishing, Paris, http://dx.doi.org/10.1787/eco_outlook-v2014-1-en. [92]

OECD (2012), *Closing the Gender Gap: Act Now*, OECD Publishing, Paris, http://dx.doi.org/10.1787/9789264179370-en. [19]

OECD (2011), *Society at a Glance 2011: OECD Social Indicators*, OECD Publishing, Paris, http://dx.doi.org/10.1787/soc_glance-2011-en. [95]

OECD (2005), *Babies and Bosses - Reconciling Work and Family Life (Volume 4): Canada, Finland, Sweden and the United Kingdom*, OECD Publishing, Paris, http://dx.doi.org/10.1787/9789264009295-en. [30]

OECD (2002), *Babies and Bosses - Reconciling Work and Family Life (Volume 1): Australia, Denmark and the Netherlands*, OECD Publishing, Paris, http://dx.doi.org/10.1787/9789264161139-en. [68]

OECD, A. et al. (2014), *Achieving stronger growth by promoting a more gender- balanced economy*, Report prepared for the G20 Labour and Employment Ministerial Meeting Melbourne, Australia, 10-11 September 2014, http://www.oecd.org/g20/topics/employment-and-social-policy/ILO-IMF-OECD-WBG-Achieving-stronger-growth-by-promoting-a-more-gender-balanced-economy-G20.pdf (accessed on 08 March 2018). [20]

Ólafsdóttir, K. and S. Ólafsson (2014), *Economy, Politics and Welfare in Iceland*, http://www.fafo.no/images/pub/2014/20360.pdf (accessed on 04 April 2018). [91]

Olivetti, C. and B. Petrongolo (2017), "The Economic Consequences of Family Policies: Lessons from a Century of Legislation in High-Income Countries", *NBER Working Paper*, No. 23051, National Bureau of Economic Research, Cambridge, United States, http://www.nber.org/papers/w23051 (accessed on 16 December 2017). [74]

Østbakken, K. (2016), *Likestilling og verdiskaping : om kvinners yrkesdeltakelse og dens betydning for økonomisk vekst*, https://brage.bibsys.no/xmlui/handle/11250/2442440 (accessed on 19 March 2018). [15]

Pareliussen, J. et al. (2018), "Income Inequality in the Nordics from an OECD Perspective", *Nordic Economic Policy Review*, pp. 17-57, http://dx.doi.org/10.6027/TN2018-519. [60]

Pedersen, A. and S. Kuhnle (2017), "Chapter: The Nordic welfare state model : 1 Introduction: The concept of a "Nordic model"", in Knutsen, I. (ed.), *The Nordic Models in Political Science : Challenged, but Still Viable?*, Fagbokforlaget, Bergen, https://brage.bibsys.no/xmlui/bitstream/handle/11250/2466194/The%20nordic%20welfare%20state_2.pdf?sequence=4 (accessed on 23 February 2018). [26]

Rønsen, M. and R. Kitterød (2015), "Gender-Equalizing Family Policies and Mothers' Entry into Paid Work: Recent Evidence From Norway", *Feminist Economics*, Vol. 21/1, pp. 59-89, http://dx.doi.org/10.1080/13545701.2014.927584. [83]

Rossin-Slater, M. (2017), "Maternity and Family Leave Policy", *IZA Discussion Paper Series*, No. 10500, http://ftp.iza.org/dp10500.pdf (accessed on 28 November 2017). [78]

Scarpetta, S. et al. (2000), "Economic Growth in the OECD Area: Recent Trends at the Aggregate and Sectoral Level", *OECD Economics Department Working Papers*, No. 248, OECD Publishing, Paris, http://dx.doi.org/10.1787/843888182178. [87]

Shorrocks, A. (2013), "Decomposition procedures for distributional analysis: a unified framework based on the Shapley value", *The Journal of Economic Inequality*, Vol. 11/1, pp. 99-126, http://dx.doi.org/10.1007/s10888-011-9214-z. [93]

Sigurdardottir, H. and Ó. Garðarsdóttir (2018), "Backlash in gender equality? Fathers' parental leave during a time of economic crisis", *Journal of European Social Policy*, p. 095892871773924, http://dx.doi.org/10.1177/0958928717739243. [82]

Skolverket (2011), *Curriculum for the Preschool Lpfö 98 Revised 2010*, ISBN 978-91-38325-75-9, https://www.skolverket.se/om-skolverket/andra-sprak/in-english/publication/2.5845?_xurl_=http%3A%2F%2Fwww5.skolverket.se%2Fwtpub%2Fws [38]

%2Fskolbok%2Fwpubext%2Ftrycksak%2FRecord%3Frpp%3D20%26upp%3D0%26m%3D1%26w%3DNATIVE%2528%2527multi%2Bph%2Bwords%2B%2527%252 (accessed on 16 February 2018).

Solow, R. (1956), "A Contribution to the Theory of Economic Growth", *The Quarterly Journal of Economics*, Vol. 70/1, p. 65, http://dx.doi.org/10.2307/1884513. [86]

Statistics Canada (2018), *Statistics Canada*, http://www.statcan.gc.ca/eng/start (accessed on 20 April 2018). [98]

Statistics Norway (2018), *Statistics Norway*, https://www.ssb.no/en/ (accessed on 20 April 2018). [113]

Statistics Sweden (2016), *Women and men in Sweden: Facts and figures 2016*, Statistics Sweden, Örebro, https://www.scb.se/Statistik/_Publikationer/LE0201_2015B16_BR_X10BR1601ENG.pdf (accessed on 12 April 2018). [2]

Stoet, G. and D. Geary (2018), "The Gender-Equality Paradox in Science, Technology, Engineering, and Mathematics Education", *Psychological Science*, p. 095679761774171, http://dx.doi.org/10.1177/0956797617741719. [36]

Stotsky, J. (2006), "Gender and Its Relevance to Macroeconomic Policy: A Survey", *IMF Working Paper*, No. WP/06/233, IMF, https://www.imf.org/external/pubs/ft/wp/2006/wp06233.pdf (accessed on 18 February 2018). [85]

Teigen, M. and H. Skjeie (2017), "The Nordic Gender Equality Model", in Knutsen, O. (ed.), *The Nordic Models in Political Science. Challenged, but Still Viable?*, Fagbokforlaget, Bergen, https://brage.bibsys.no/xmlui/bitstream/handle/11250/2467492/The%2bNordic%2bGender%2bEquality%2bModel%2bChap%2b5.pdf?sequence=4&isAllowed=y (accessed on 04 April 2018). [6]

Thévenon, O. (2013), "Drivers of Female Labour Force Participation in the OECD", *OECD Social, Employment and Migration Working Papers*, No. 145, OECD Publishing, Paris, http://dx.doi.org/10.1787/5k46cvrgnms6-en. [72]

Thévenon, O. (2011), "Family Policies in OECD Countries: A Comparative Analysis", *Population and Development Review*, Vol. 37/1, pp. 57-87, http://dx.doi.org/10.1111/j.1728-4457.2011.00390.x. [22]

Thévenon, O. and A. Solaz (2013), "Labour Market Effects of Parental Leave Policies in OECD Countries", *OECD Social, Employment and Migration Working Papers*, No. 141, OECD Publishing, Paris, http://dx.doi.org/10.1787/5k8xb6hw1wjf-en. [80]

Van de Velde, S. et al. (2013), "Macro-level gender equality and depression in men and women in Europe", *Sociology of Health & Illness*, Vol. 35/5, pp. 682-698, http://dx.doi.org/10.1111/j.1467-9566.2012.01521.x. [8]

Annex A. Additional tables and figures

The statistical data for Israel are supplied by and under the responsibility of the relevant Israeli authorities. The use of such data by the OECD is without prejudice to the status of the Golan Heights, East Jerusalem and Israeli settlements in the West Bank under the terms of international law.

Figure A A.1. Men's employment has been declining slowly for decades

Male employment rate, 15-64 year-olds, 1960-2016, selected OECD countries

Panel A. Nordic OECD member countries

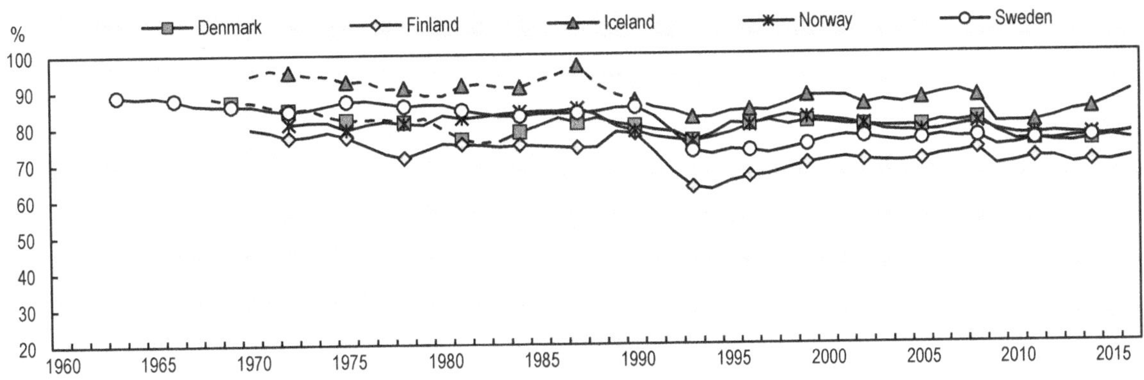

Panel B. Selected other OECD member countries

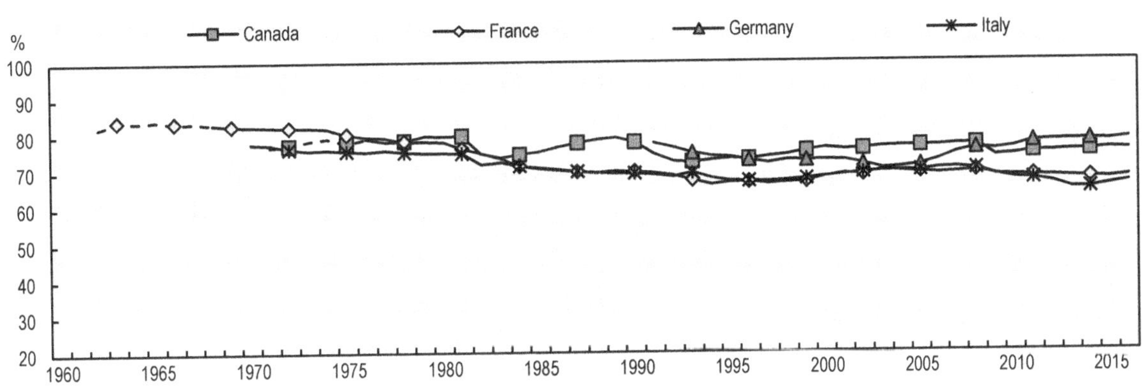

Panel C. Selected other OECD member countries (cont.)

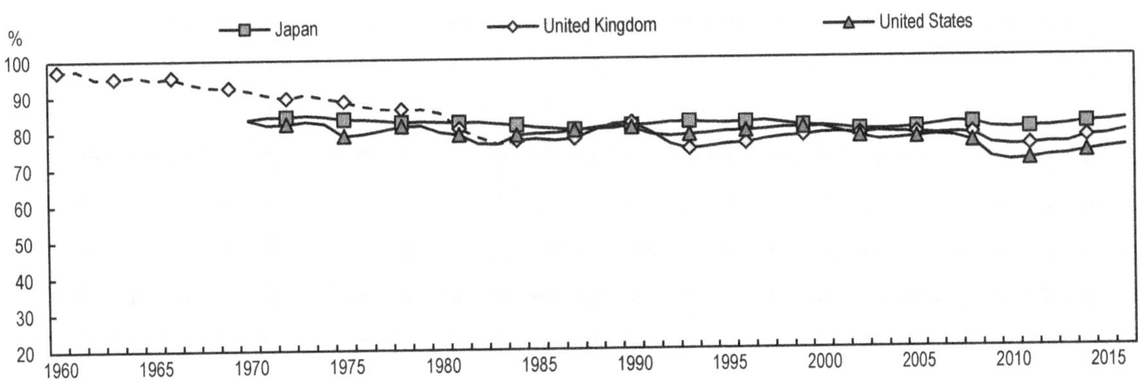

Note: Dashed lines reflect estimated data points (see Annex B).
Source: *OECD Employment Database* (http://www.oecd.org/employment/emp/onlineoecdemploymentdatabase.htm), and OECD estimates based on data from the *OECD Annual Labour Force Statistics Database* (http://stats.oecd.org/index.aspx?queryid=451), Eurostat (http://ec.europa.eu/eurostat/data/database), and national statistical offices (see Annex B).

Figure A A.2. Men's average working hours have decreased, especially in Denmark and Iceland

Male average usual weekly working hours, all ages, 1975-2016, selected OECD countries

Panel A. Nordic OECD member countries

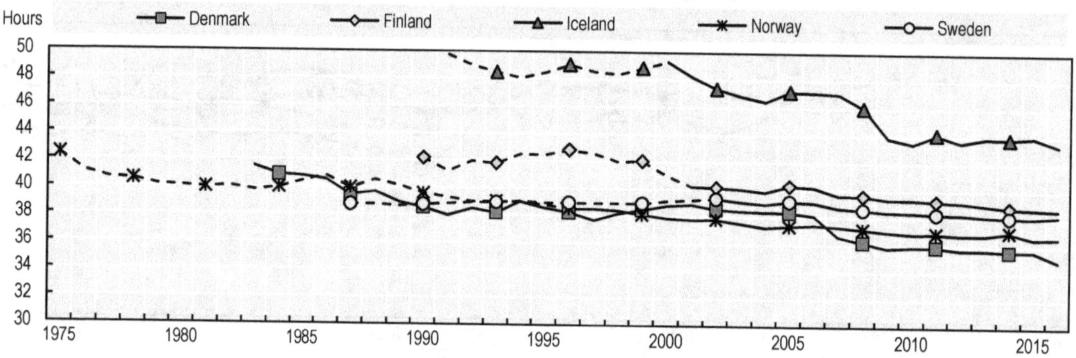

Panel B. Selected other OECD member countries

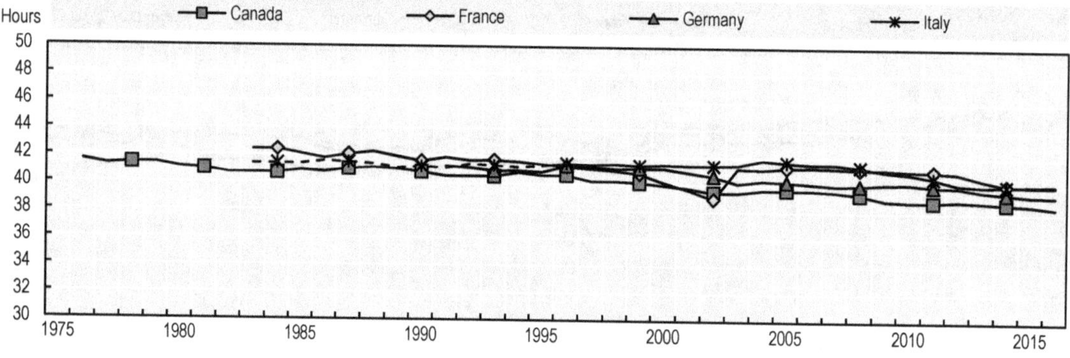

Panel C. Selected other OECD member countries (cont.)

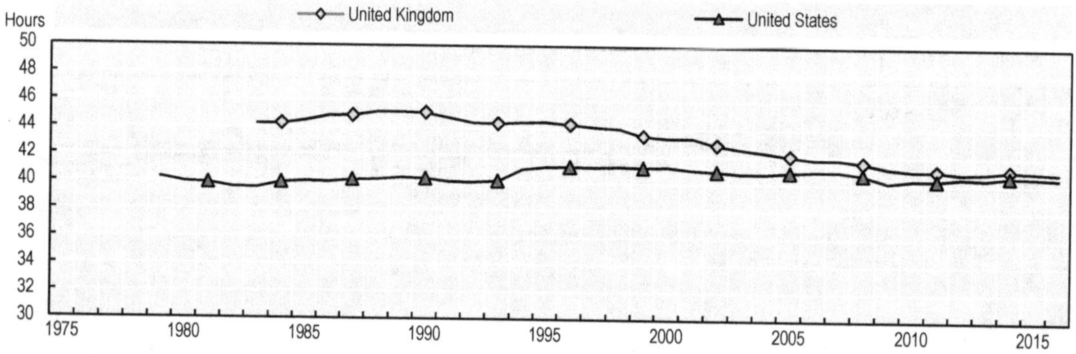

Note: Data refer to average usual weekly working hours in the main job, and cover all employed (both employees and self-employed) of all ages. Data for the United States refer to dependent employees, only. Dashed lines reflect estimated data points (see Annex B for details).

Source: *OECD Employment Database* (http://www.oecd.org/employment/emp/onlineoecdemploymentdatabase.htm), and OECD estimates based on data from the *OECD Annual Labour Force Statistics Database* (http://stats.oecd.org/index.aspx?queryid=451), Eurostat (http://ec.europa.eu/eurostat/data/database), and national statistical offices (see Annex B).

Figure A A.3. All of the Nordic countries have seen large increases in GDP per capita over the past 50 years or so

GDP per capita, constant prices, constant PPPs, OECD base year (USD 2010), 1960-2016

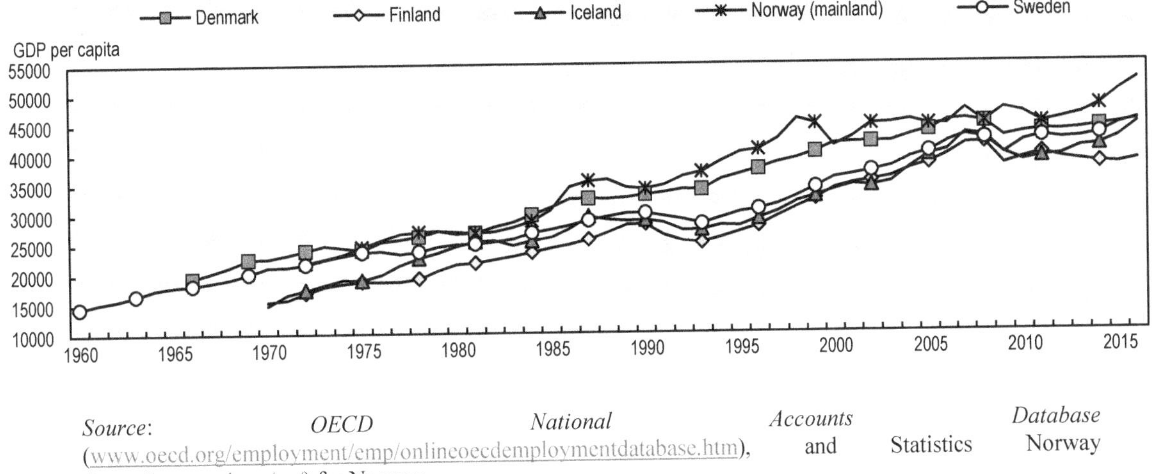

Source: *OECD National Accounts Database* (www.oecd.org/employment/emp/onlineoecdemploymentdatabase.htm), and Statistics Norway (https://www.ssb.no/en/) for Norway.

Table A A.1. In the Nordic countries, gender employment gaps tend to fall around the time of economic crises but widen again during the recovery

Employment rates in the Nordic countries around the time of the early-1990s economic crisis (Finland and Sweden) and the Great Recession (Denmark, Iceland and Norway), 15-64 year-olds, by gender

		1989	1990	1991	1992	1993	1994	1995	1996	1997	1998
Finland	Male	78.4	77.9	73.0	67.3	63.1	62.6	64.8	66.0	66.6	68.2
	Female	71.4	71.5	68.4	63.8	59.7	58.7	59.0	59.5	60.4	61.3
	Gender gap	7.1	6.4	4.6	3.5	3.4	3.8	5.8	6.5	6.2	6.8
Sweden	Male	85.1	85.2	82.7	78.2	73.1	72.2	73.5	73.2	72.4	73.6
	Female	80.7	81.0	79.3	76.2	72.1	70.7	70.9	69.9	68.9	69.4
	Gender gap	4.4	4.3	3.4	1.9	1.0	1.6	2.6	3.3	3.5	4.2
		2007	2008	2009	2010	2011	2012	2013	2014	2015	2016
Denmark	Male	80.8	81.6	78.0	75.6	75.9	75.2	75.0	75.8	76.6	77.7
	Female	73.2	74.1	72.7	71.1	70.4	70.0	70.0	69.8	70.4	72.0
	Gender gap	7.6	7.5	5.3	4.5	5.5	5.2	5.0	6.0	6.2	5.7
Iceland	Male	89.5	87.8	80.6	80.6	80.8	81.9	83.7	84.4	86.6	89.0
	Female	81.7	80.3	77.2	77.0	77.3	78.5	79.9	80.0	81.8	83.4
	Gender gap	7.8	7.5	3.4	3.6	3.5	3.4	3.7	4.4	4.8	5.6
Norway	Male	79.7	80.6	78.4	77.4	77.2	77.7	77.4	77.1	76.6	75.8
	Female	74.0	75.4	74.4	73.3	73.4	73.8	73.5	73.4	73.0	72.8
	Gender gap	5.6	5.2	4.0	4.1	3.8	3.9	3.9	3.7	3.6	3.0

Source: *OECD Employment Database* (www.oecd.org/employment/emp/onlineoecdemploymentdatabase.htm).

Table A A.2. Except for in Iceland, gender working hours gaps in the Nordic countries have changed little around the times of recession

Average usual weekly working hours in the Nordic countries around the time of the early-1990s economic crisis (Finland and Sweden) and the Great Recession (Denmark, Iceland and Norway), all ages, total employment, by gender

		1989	1990	1991	1992	1993	1994	1995	1996	1997	1998
Finland	Male	..	42.2*	41.2*	42.0*	41.8*	42.5*	42.4*	42.8*	42.5*	42.0*
	Female	..	36.8*	36.9*	37.1*	36.2*	37.2*	36.9*	37.3*	37.1*	36.8*
	Gender gap	..	5.3*	4.3*	4.9*	5.6*	5.3*	5.6*	5.5*	5.4*	5.2*
Sweden	Male	38.6*	38.7*	38.8*	38.9*	38.9*	39.0*	38.9*	38.9*	38.9*	38.9*
	Female	35.5*	35.2*	35.3*	35.4*	35.5*	35.4*	35.2*	35.1*	34.9*	34.7*
	Gender gap	3.1*	3.5*	3.5*	3.5*	3.4*	3.6*	3.7*	3.8*	4.0*	4.2*

		2007	2008	2009	2010	2011	2012	2013	2014	2015	2016
Denmark	Male	36.6	36.2	35.8	35.9	35.9	35.7	35.7	35.6	35.6	34.9
	Female	31.8	31.7	31.4	31.2	31.2	31.2	31.3	31.1	31.0	30.6
	Gender gap	4.8	4.5	4.4	4.7	4.7	4.4	4.4	4.5	4.6	4.2
Iceland	Male	47.0	46.0	43.8	43.4	44.1	43.6	43.9	43.8	43.9	43.3
	Female	35.2	35.5	34.5	34.4	34.9	35.0	34.9	35.2	35.0	34.9
	Gender gap	11.8	10.5	9.3	9.1	9.2	8.6	9.0	8.6	8.9	8.4
Norway	Male	37.3	37.1	37.0	36.8	36.9	36.8	36.8	37.0	36.5	36.6
	Female	30.8	31.1	31.1	31.1	31.1	31.5	31.4	31.6	31.6	31.8
	Gender gap	6.5	6.1	5.8	5.8	5.7	5.3	5.3	5.4	4.9	4.8

Note: Data refer to average usual weekly working hours in the main job, and cover all employed (both employees and self-employed) of all ages. Data points marked with an * refer to estimated data (see Annex B).

Source: *OECD* *Employment* *Database* (http://www.oecd.org/employment/emp/onlineoecdemploymentdatabase.htm), and OECD estimates based on data from national statistical offices (see Annex B).

Table A A.3. Increases in women's employment have contributed to economic growth in the Nordic countries

Average annual rate of growth in GDP per capita and disaggregation of growth into its primary components, longest available series, Nordic and selected other OECD member countries

	GDP per capita, average annual growth rate (%)	Percentage point contribution of main components			Decomposition of contribution of the employment rate, by gender	
		Labour productivity (p.p.)	Working age share of population (p.p.)	Employment rate (p.p.)	Men's employment (p.p.)	Women's employment (p.p.)
Denmark (1967-2016)	1.64	1.55	0.00	0.09	-0.15	0.24
Finland (1970-2016)	2.01	2.19	-0.12	-0.06	-0.12	0.05
Iceland (1970-2016)	2.42	1.83	0.20	0.40	0.00	0.40
Norway (mainland) (1972-2016)	1.99	1.46	0.16	0.36	-0.05	0.41
Sweden (1963-2016)	1.92	1.93	-0.07	0.06	-0.19	0.25
Canada (1971-2016)	1.58	1.01	0.15	0.41	-0.06	0.48
France (1962-2016)	2.06	2.09	-0.05	0.01	-0.25	0.26
Germany (1991-2016)	1.24	0.88	-0.22	0.58	0.11	0.47
Italy (1970-2016)	1.46	1.24	-0.04	0.26	-0.17	0.43
Japan (1970-2015)	2.10	2.13	-0.31	0.28	0.07	0.21
United Kingdom (1960-2016)	1.97	1.84	-0.01	0.14	-0.19	0.32
United States (1970-2016)	1.77	1.41	0.22	0.14	-0.12	0.26

Note: Estimates based on the decomposition of national accounts data using labour force survey estimates. Differences in the time periods covered mean estimates are not fully comparable across countries. See Annex B for more detail.
Source: OECD estimates based on data from the *OECD National Accounts Database* (http://www.oecd.org/std/na/), the *OECD Employment Database* (http://www.oecd.org/employment/emp/onlineoecdemploymentdatabase.htm), the European Commission's *AMECO Database* (http://ec.europa.eu/economy_finance/ameco/user/serie/SelectSerie.cfm), Eurostat (http://ec.europa.eu/eurostat/data/database), and national statistical offices (see Annex B).

Table A A.4. Most of the gains from women's employment have come from 25-54 year-old women, but 55-64 year-old women have contributed too

Average annual rate of growth in GDP per capita and disaggregation of growth into its primary components, with the contribution of women's employment disaggregated by age group, longest available series, Nordic and selected other OECD member countries

	GDP per capita, average annual growth rate (%)	Percentage point contribution of main components			Decomposition of the contribution of the employment rate, by gender		Disaggregation of the contribution of women's employment by age group		
		Labour productivity (p.p.)	Working age share of population (p.p.)	Employment rate (p.p.)	Men's employment (p.p.)	Women's employment (p.p.)	15-24 year-olds (p.p.)	25-54 year-olds (p.p.)	55-64 year-olds (p.p.)
Denmark (1983-2016)	1.39	1.29	-0.07	0.16	0.03	0.14	0.00	0.02	0.12
Finland (1970-2016)	2.01	2.19	-0.12	-0.06	-0.12	0.05	-0.13	0.08	0.10
Iceland (1991-2016)	1.82	1.56	-0.05	0.31	0.10	0.20	0.01	0.08	0.11
Norway (mainland) (1972-2016)	1.99	1.46	0.16	0.36	-0.05	0.41	0.00	0.34	0.08
Sweden (1963-2016)	1.92	1.93	-0.07	0.06	-0.19	0.25	-0.06	0.23	0.08
Canada (1976-2016)	1.37	0.89	0.04	0.44	-0.02	0.46	-0.09	0.40	0.15
France (1968-2016)	1.78	1.74	0.00	0.04	-0.25	0.29	-0.12	0.36	0.05
Germany (1991-2016)	1.24	0.88	-0.22	0.58	0.11	0.47	-0.07	0.27	0.28
Italy (1970-2016)	1.46	1.24	-0.04	0.26	-0.17	0.43	-0.11	0.39	0.15
Japan (1970-2015)	2.10	2.13	-0.31	0.28	0.07	0.21	-0.13	0.22	0.12
United Kingdom (1984-2016)	1.82	1.44	-0.05	0.42	0.06	0.37	-0.07	0.33	0.11
United States (1970-2016)	1.77	1.41	0.22	0.14	-0.12	0.26	-0.06	0.24	0.08

Note: Estimates based on the decomposition of national accounts data using labour force survey estimates. Differences in the time periods covered mean estimates are not fully comparable across countries. See Annex B for more detail.

Source: OECD estimates based on data from the *OECD National Accounts Database* (http://www.oecd.org/std/na/), the *OECD Employment Database* (http://www.oecd.org/employment/emp/onlineoecdemploymentdatabase.htm), the European Commission's *AMECO Database* (http://ec.europa.eu/economy_finance/ameco/user/serie/SelectSerie.cfm), Eurostat (http://ec.europa.eu/eurostat/data/database), and national statistical offices (see Annex B).

Table A A.5. Growth in women's working hours have contributed relatively little to economic growth in the Nordic countries

Average annual rate of growth in GDP per capita and disaggregation of growth into its primary components, employment rates and working hours, longest available series, Nordic and selected other OECD member countries

		Percentage point contribution of main components				Decomposition of the contribution of the employment rate, by gender		Decomposition of the contribution of working hours, by gender	
	GDP per capita, average annual growth rate (%)	Labour productivity (p.p.)	Working age share of population (p.p.)	Employment rate (p.p.)	Working hours (p.p.)	Men's employment (p.p.)	Women's employment (p.p.)	Men's working hours (p.p.)	Women's working hours (p.p.)
Denmark (1983-2016)	1.39	1.58	-0.07	0.17	-0.29	0.03	0.14	-0.33	0.04
Finland (1990-2016)	1.21	1.85	-0.26	-0.07	-0.31	-0.06	-0.01	-0.22	-0.09
Iceland (1991-2016)	1.82	1.82	-0.05	0.31	-0.26	0.11	0.20	-0.41	0.15
Norway (mainland) (1975-2016)	1.86	1.85	0.13	0.38	-0.50	-0.03	0.41	-0.66	0.16
Sweden (1987-2016)	1.56	1.66	-0.03	-0.21	0.15	-0.12	-0.10	0.11	0.04
Canada (1976-2016)	1.37	2.08	0.04	0.47	-1.22	-0.02	0.49	-1.08	-0.14
France (1983-2016)	1.25	1.52	-0.19	0.25	-0.33	-0.11	0.36	-0.44	0.10
Germany (1991-2016)	1.24	1.43	-0.23	0.58	-0.55	0.11	0.47	-0.47	-0.08
Italy (1983-2016)	0.97	1.00	-0.19	0.41	-0.25	-0.05	0.46	-0.44	0.19
United Kingdom (1984-2016)	1.82	1.70	-0.05	0.43	-0.26	0.06	0.37	-0.44	0.19
United States (1979-2016)	1.60	2.39	0.04	0.10	-0.93	-0.09	0.20	-0.73	-0.20

Note: Estimates based on the decomposition of national accounts data using labour force survey estimates. Differences in the time periods covered mean estimates are not fully comparable across countries. See Annex B for more detail.

Source: OECD estimates based on data from the *OECD National Accounts Database* (http://www.oecd.org/std/na/), the *OECD Employment Database* (http://www.oecd.org/employment/emp/onlineoecdemploymentdatabase.htm), the European Commission's *AMECO Database* (http://ec.europa.eu/economy_finance/ameco/user/serie/SelectSerie.cfm), Eurostat (http://ec.europa.eu/eurostat/data/database), and national statistical offices (see Annex B).

Table A A.6. The relatively high levels of female employment in the Nordic countries contribute to their relative prosperity

Gap in GDP per capita relative to the OECD-30 total and decomposition of the gap into its primary components, USD 2010 PPP, 2015, Nordic and selected other OECD member countries

		Percentage point contribution of main components				Decomposition of the contribution of the employment rate, by gender		Decomposition of the contribution of working hours, by gender	
	Difference in GDP per capita (USD)	Labour productivity (USD)	Working age share of population (USD)	Employment rate (USD)	Average working hours (USD)	Men's employment (USD)	Women's employment (USD)	Men's working hours (USD)	Women's working hours (USD)
Denmark	2 429.0	7 736.1	- 136.8	2 994.7	-8 165.0	1 115.2	1 879.5	-5 301.9	-2 863.1
Finland	-4 226.9	-1 839.6	- 564.4	- 244.7	-1 578.1	-1 066.1	821.3	-2 337.5	759.3
Iceland	135.0	-11 519.5	-1 281.4	8 727.4	4 208.5	3 817.7	4 909.6	2 370.8	1 837.7
Norway (mainland)	8 014.5	11 780.7	1 002.8	3 910.5	-8 679.6	1 539.2	2 371.3	-5 619.9	-3 059.7
Sweden	2 228.0	2 460.7	- 955.5	3 154.3	-2 431.5	912.6	2 241.7	-2 729.3	297.7
Canada	322.6	-3 556.9	1 293.6	2 489.1	96.7	669.4	1 819.7	- 528.9	625.6
France	-5 176.3	4 489.2	-2 959.4	-1 933.7	-4 772.3	-1 828.1	- 105.7	-3 516.3	-1 256.0
Germany	575.8	4 678.4	337.2	4 904.0	-9 343.7	2 383.3	2 520.7	-4 654.3	-4 689.4
Italy	-8 844.5	-3 740.2	- 30.3	-5 399.9	325.8	-1 428.7	-3 971.2	2 124.6	-1 798.7
United Kingdom	-3 733.2	-3 845.9	-1 140.1	2 347.0	-1 094.2	927.4	1 419.6	- 1.9	-1 092.2
United States	9 816.6	8 190.7	- 527.7	917.8	1 235.8	202.6	715.2	- 172.4	1 408.2

Note: Estimates based on the decomposition of national accounts data using labour force survey estimates. Differences in definitions and the data used mean estimates are not fully comparable across countries. See Annex B for more details

Source: OECD estimates based on data from the *OECD National Accounts Database* (http://www.oecd.org/std/na/), the *OECD Employment Database* (http://www.oecd.org/employment/emp/onlineoecdemploymentdatabase.htm), the European Commission's *AMECO Database* (http://ec.europa.eu/economy_finance/ameco/user/serie/SelectSerie.cfm), Eurostat (http://ec.europa.eu/eurostat/data/database), and national statistical offices (see Annex B)

Table A A.7. Potential gains from closing gender participation gaps are fairly small in the Nordic countries, but closing working hours gaps could lead to larger gains

Projected GDP per capita and projected average annual rate of growth in GDP per capita under different gender gap scenarios, 2013-2040, OECD countries

		Projected GDP per capita, 2040, USD 2005 PPP						Average annual rate of growth in GDP per capita, 2013-2040, %					
Labour force participation scenario:	GDP per capita, 2012, USD 2005 PPP	Baseline	25% by 2025, 50% by 2040	50% by 2025, 100% by 2040	25% by 2025, 50% by 2040	25% by 2025, 50% by 2040	50% by 2025, 100% by 2040	Baseline	25% by 2025, 50% by 2040	50% by 2025, 100% by 2040	25% by 2025, 50% by 2040	25% by 2025, 50% by 2040	50% by 2025, 100% by 2040
Working hours scenario:		Baseline	Baseline	Baseline	25% by 2025, 50% by 2040	25% by 2025, 50% by 2040 (male driven)	50% by 2025, 100% by 2040	Baseline	Baseline	Baseline	25% by 2025, 50% by 2040	25% by 2025, 50% by 2040 (male driven)	50% by 2025, 100% by 2040
Denmark	32 393.1	50 739.6	51 755.9	52 524.1	52 753.3	50 642.1	56 881.3	1.62	1.69	1.74	1.76	1.61	2.03
Finland	31 634.7	50 983.3	51 214.4	51 704.2	52 076.2	49 918.5	54 886.9	1.72	1.74	1.77	1.8	1.64	1.99
Iceland	33 301.3	49 277.9	49 163.5	49 673.7	50 722.3	46 439.4	54 831.8	1.41	1.4	1.44	1.51	1.19	1.8
Norway	56 441.5	82 195.4	82 727.7	83 715.9	84 460.3	80 152.3	90 432.1	1.35	1.37	1.42	1.45	1.26	1.7
Sweden	35 067.5	59 157.6	59 351.5	59 971.5	60 249.4	57 992.4	63 491.2	1.89	1.9	1.93	1.95	1.81	2.14
Canada	37 068.1	53 050.4	53 858.4	54 741.2	55 122.	52 252.5	60 058.4	1.29	1.34	1.4	1.43	1.23	1.74
France	29 949.1	48 205.4	48 559.3	49 529.6	49 588.7	47 095.	54 030.1	1.71	1.74	1.81	1.82	1.63	2.13
Germany	35 039.3	51 489.9	51 495.5	52 545.5	53 347.6	48 395.7	59 698.2	1.38	1.38	1.46	1.51	1.16	1.92
Italy	26 325.8	39 170.1	39 408.3	41 294.8	40 571.5	37 353.2	46 509.2	1.43	1.45	1.62	1.56	1.26	2.05
Japan	31 398.5	48 051.2	48 203.3	50 484.3	..	..	..	1.53	1.54	1.71	..	..	..
United Kingdom	32 910.9	57 048.6	57 746.7	59 074.3	59 870.5	54 552.4	67 609.9	1.98	2.03	2.11	2.16	1.82	2.6
United States	44 832.5	71 706.6	72 425.	74 404.6	73 535.1	70 974.1	79 726.6	1.69	1.73	1.83	1.78	1.65	2.08
Australia	36 574.1	63 510.	64 255.8	65 894.3	66 444.5	61 001.7	75 400.5	1.99	2.03	2.12	2.16	1.84	2.62
Austria	36 388.	58 011.	57 859.7	59 001.6	59 951.7	54 402.6	66 735.3	1.68	1.67	1.74	1.8	1.45	2.19
Belgium	33 045.7	50 645.8	51 148.2	52 441.	52 605.1	49 011.5	58 656.6	1.54	1.57	1.66	1.67	1.42	2.07
Chile	15 842.5	38 355.	38 147.4	40 493.1	38 954.3	36 572.2	44 776.3	3.21	3.19	3.41	3.27	3.03	3.78
Czech Republic	23 655.1	47 974.8	49 214.1	50 788.5	49 806.1	48 814.3	54 445.1	2.56	2.65	2.77	2.69	2.62	3.02
Estonia	18 943.8	41 405.5	42 173.7	42 650.8	42 465.8	42 077.9	44 527.8	2.83	2.9	2.94	2.92	2.89	3.1

Greece	20 626.2	39 304.6	38 639.9	40 417.9	39 397.1	36 937.5	43 454.5	2.33	2.27	2.43	2.34	2.1	2.7
Hungary	16 932.6	30 359.2	31 414.8	32 091.9	31 561.5	31 716.1	33 619.8	2.11	2.23	2.31	2.25	2.27	2.48
Ireland	36 662.7	54 969.4	54 087.	55 975.2	56 100.1	50 226.4	63 391.2	1.46	1.4	1.52	1.53	1.13	1.97
Israel	30 001.6	48 707.7	48 406.7	49 433.2	49 745.5	46 063.4	54 656.7	1.75	1.72	1.8	1.82	1.54	2.17
Korea	30 870.3	59 549.1	61 198.7	64 171.2	62 398.5	59 805.4	70 633.6	2.37	2.47	2.65	2.55	2.39	3
Luxembourg	67 356.5	95 187.6	94 449.7	97 157.2	96 570.	90 669.3	106 177.6	1.24	1.21	1.32	1.29	1.07	1.64
Mexico	12 992.1	24 536.8	26 141.2	28 312.1	26 936.7	25 596.6	33 692.1	2.3	2.53	2.82	2.64	2.45	3.46
Netherlands	36 525.7	61 846.9	62 073.8	63 303.2	65 201.	57 090.6	74 993.2	1.9	1.91	1.98	2.09	1.61	2.6
New Zealand	26 114.	42 383.2	42 778.	43 704.5	44 257.2	40 493.5	43 958.8	1.74	1.78	1.86	1.9	1.58	1.88
Poland	18 446.2	32 680.	33 643.3	34 635.9	34 069.4	33 414.3	37 340.	2.06	2.17	2.28	2.22	2.14	2.55
Portugal	20 768.3	35 785.7	35 894.8	36 742.3	36 301.2	35 312.8	38 805.9	1.96	1.97	2.06	2.01	1.91	2.26
Slovak Republic	21 023.5	39 225.1	40 450.8	41 752.2	40 814.	40 447.1	44 311.3	2.25	2.36	2.48	2.4	2.36	2.7
Slovenia	24 255.3	41 003.3	41 889.9	42 578.4	42 307.4	41 658.7	44 758.3	1.89	1.97	2.03	2.01	1.95	2.21
Spain	26 318.7	38 033.1	37 563.3	38 546.8	38 395.	35 993.5	41 713.4	1.32	1.28	1.37	1.36	1.12	1.66
Switzerland	39 491.5	60 289.1	60 426.3	61 871.8	..	..	..	1.52	1.53	1.62	..	..	..
Turkey	13 722.3	32 257.4	33 174.8	36 177.8	33 715.8	32 498.2	41 516.	3.1	3.2	3.52	3.26	3.13	4.03
United Kingdom	32 910.9	57 048.6	57 746.7	59 074.3	59 870.5	54 552.4	67 609.9	1.98	2.03	2.11	2.16	1.82	2.6
United States	44 832.5	71 706.6	72 425.	74 404.6	73 535.1	70 974.1	79 726.6	1.69	1.73	1.83	1.78	1.65	2.08

Note: Projections using adjustments to working hours not available for Japan and Switzerland due to missing data on average usual weekly working hours. For the United States, working hours data based on dependent employees only. See Annex B for a description of the method and data used.

Source: OECD estimates based on OECD (2014), *OECD Economic Outlook No. 95 Volume 2014 Issue 1*, OECD Publishing, Paris (http://dx.doi.org/10.1787/eco_outlook-v2014-1-en), *OECD Economic Outlook: Statistics and Projections Databases* (http://stats.oecd.org/index.aspx?dataSetCode=EO), OECD population data and the *OECD Employment Database* (http://www.oecd.org/employment/emp/onlineoecdemploymentdatabase.htm).

Annex B. Methods and data

This annex provides details of the methods and data used in the empirical exercises presented in Sections 3 and 4. It starts with a description of the methods and data used in the growth accounting exercises in Sections 3.1 and 3.2, followed by a similar description for the development accounting exercise in Section 3.3 and, lastly, an overview of the methods used for the forward-looking projections in Section 4.

Growth accounting estimates in Sections 3.1 and 3.2

The analyses presented in Sections 3.1 and 3.2 are based primarily on growth accounting – a procedure used to identify and decompose the sources of economic growth. Using macro-economic time-series, the basic principle of growth accounting is to split economic growth into its main components parts under standard macroeconomic theory: labour, capital, and total factor productivity (Solow, 1956[86]). Data permitting, the contribution of each of these main components can then be further decomposed into sub-components, as required.

Theoretical model

The starting point for the growth accounting exercise is a standard Cobb-Douglas production function with constant returns to scale. Total economic output, measured by Gross Domestic Product (GDP), can be expressed using the following multiplicative function:

$$Y = K^{1-\alpha}.\left(A.Q.E.\frac{H}{E}\right)^{\alpha} \tag{1}$$

where Y is GDP, K is physical capital, A is technological progress, Q is human capital per person employed, E is headcount employment, H is total hours worked (and therefore, H/E hours worked per person employed), and α is the labour share of output.

After some manipulations, this can be re-written as:

$$Y = \left(\frac{K}{Y}\right)^{(1-\alpha)/\alpha}.A.Q.E.\frac{H}{E} \tag{2}$$

and output per person, measured by GDP per capita, can be expressed as:

$$\frac{Y}{P} = \left(\frac{K}{Y}\right)^{(1-\alpha)/\alpha}.A.Q.\frac{WP}{P}.\frac{E}{WP}.\frac{H}{E} \tag{3}$$

where P stands for the population and WP for the working-age population, Y/P is GDP per capita, K/Y is the capital-to-output ratio, WP/P is the working-age share of the population, and E/WP is the employment-to-working-age-population ratio, or employment rate. Note that, in this particular model, employment is limited to those of working-age (15-64 year-olds) only. This is to allow for better modelling of how shifts in the working-age share of the population contribute to output.

A useful manipulation here is to split GDP per capita into the product of labour utilisation (covering the working-age share of the population, the employment-to-working-age-population ratio, and hours worked per person employed), and labour productivity or output per hour worked, covering all other factors (physical capital, technological progress, and human capital):

$$\frac{Y}{P} = \left(\frac{Y}{E.H}\right) \cdot \left(\frac{WP}{P} \cdot \frac{E}{WP} \cdot \frac{H}{E}\right) \qquad (4)$$

where:

$$\frac{Y}{E.H} = \left(\frac{K}{Y}\right)^{(1-\alpha)/\alpha} . A . Q \qquad (5)$$

Labour utilisation can also itself be split into its component parts. The focus here is on disaggregating the employment rate (E/WP) and hours worked per person employed (H/E) by gender and, where possible, age group, as expressed by the following two additive functions:

$$\frac{E}{WP} = \Sigma_{G \in \{(15-24)men,(15-24),women,(25-54)men,(25-54)women,(55-64)men,(55-64)women\}} \frac{E_G}{WP} \qquad (6)$$

And

$$\frac{H}{E} = \Sigma_{G \in \{(15-24)men,(15-24),women,(25-54)men,(25-54)women,(55-64)men,(55-64)women\}} \frac{H_G}{E} \qquad (7)$$

Lastly, the model shown in equation 4 can be re-written in growth rates to give changes in economic output over time, as expressed by the following additive function:

$$g_{\frac{Y}{P}} = g_{\left(\frac{Y}{E.H}\right)} + g_{\frac{WP}{P}} + g_{\frac{E}{WP}} + g_{\frac{H}{E}} \qquad (8)$$

where the g is the growth rate for the given factor, and with growth rates for the employment rate (g[E/WP]) and hours worked per person employed (g[H/E]) themselves calculated as

$$g_{\frac{E}{WP}} = \Sigma_{G \in \{(15-24)men,(15-24),women,(25-54)men,(25-54)women,(55-64)men,(55-64)women\}} g_{\frac{E_G}{WP}} \qquad (9)$$

and

$$g_{\frac{H}{E}} = \Sigma_{G \in \{(15-24)men,(15-24),women,(25-54)men,(25-54)women,(55-64)men,(55-64)women\}} g_{\frac{H_G}{E}} \qquad (10)$$

It is equations 8-10 that form the core of growth accounting exercise.

Data and estimation procedure

Estimation itself is conducted using the "Shapley decomposition" (Shorrocks, 2013[93]) – a procedure initially used in the inequalities literature to identify the contribution of different income sources to income inequality, but more recently also applied to other tasks such as, for instance, the decomposition of the drivers of poverty reduction (Azevedo et al., 2013[94]). Shapley decomposition runs through all possible sequences (effectively, combinations) of a given function in order to isolate the contribution of a given component – in this case, the contributions of growth in labour productivity (Y/(E.H)), growth in the working age share of the population (WP/P), growth in the employment rate (E/WP), and growth in average hours worked per person employed (H.E). It has the advantage of producing estimates that are additive (so that, in this case, growth in GDP per capita is estimated the sum of growth in the various components) and, at least when the number of components is fairly low, is also simple to calculate. A detailed overview of the Shapley decomposition method itself can be found in Shorrocks (2013[93]).

The estimates are produced in two stages. First, growth in GDP per capita is decomposed into each of its main components – as shown in equation 8 above, growth in labour productivity (Y/(E.H)), in the working age share of the population (WP/P), in the employment rate (E/WP), and in average hours worked per person employed (H.E). Second, the contributions of growth in both the employment-to-population rate (E/WP) and in average hours worked per person employed (H.E) are then themselves decomposed by gender and, where possible, by age group too, as shown in equations 9 and 10. It is these last two decompositions (of the employment rate and of average working hours) that are where the main interest lies – they provide information on the extent to which changes in men's and especially women's employment rates and working hours have contributed to economic growth. This procedure is run separately for each country.

The data used for the growth accounting exercise are based on a combination of official macroeconomic data from national accounts databases and employment and working hours estimates from labour force surveys. Data for the first stage are taken from the *OECD National Accounts Database*. The data series used include Gross Domestic Product (GDP), total population, total employment, and average working hours per person employed (see Table A B.1 for a summary). On occasion, important series are missing in the OECD database. Where this is the case, values are imputed or interpolated using information from alternative national accounts databases, such as the European Commission's *AMECO Database* or those published by national statistical offices (see Table A B.2).

Table A B.1. Summary of data series used in Section 3

Series	Details	Main source	Additional sources
GDP (expenditure approach)	Constant prices, constant PPPs, OECD base year (USD 2010)	OECD National Accounts Database	Statistics Norway
Total population	National concept, 1000s	OECD National Accounts Database	EC AMECO Database
Total employment	Domestic concept, 1000s	OECD National Accounts Database	EC AMECO Database; Statistics Norway (SSB); OECD Employment Database
Hours worked for total employment	Domestic concept, hours, millions	OECD National Accounts Database	Statistics Norway (SSB); OECD Employment Database
Population by age and gender	1000s	OECD Employment Database	Eurostat; Statistics Canada; Statistics Iceland
Employment by age and gender	1000s	OECD Employment Database	OECD Annual Labour Force Statistics Database; National Economic Institute of Iceland
Average usual weekly working hours by age and gender	Total employment, hours	OECD Employment Database	Eurostat; Statistics Canada; Statistics Finland; Statistics Iceland; Statistics Norway; Statistics Sweden

The second stage of the growth accounting exercise requires data on population, employment, and working hours that are disaggregated by age and gender. Because national accounts databases do not typically disaggregate information by age or gender, these data are estimated using information from labour force surveys – in short, the overall national accounts series on population, employment and hours are split and *allocated* across the various gender- and age groups according to the distribution of the given series provided by labour force survey data. As our interest is largely on the working-age population only – and also because national accounts series are not always precisely consistent with estimates from labour force surveys, for various coverage, definitional and methodological reasons – the labour force survey estimates for employment and working hours are re-scaled prior to this *'allocation'*, so that the aggregated estimates for the working-age population match exactly those from the national accounts series.

The labour force survey data used for this second stage are taken primarily from the *OECD Employment Database* or from data series supplied by the Nordic national statistical offices in response to an OECD questionnaire (see Table A B.1). Where data are missing, values are imputed using information from alternative sources such as the *Eurostat Database* or alternative information from national statistical offices, or are estimated by trending the nearest observation back or forward using alternative but similar series (see Table A B.2). Even so, the length of available series differs across countries (see Box 3.2).

Table A B.2. Country-specific notes for the data series used in Section 3

Series	Country	Details
GDP (expenditure approach)	Norway	All data refer to mainland GDP only (i.e. excluding oil and gas). Data are taken from Statistics Norway.
Total population	Sweden	Data missing in the OECD National Accounts Database for years before 1970. Data for years before 1970 are estimated by trending backwards using alternative data on total population from the EC's AMECO Database.
Total employment	Iceland	Data fully missing in the OECD National Accounts Database for all years. Replaced with alternative data on total employment (domestic concept) from the EC's AMECO Database.
	Norway	All data refer to mainland employment only (i.e. excluding oil and gas). Data are taken from Statistics Norway.
	Sweden	Data missing in the OECD National Accounts Database for years before 1980. Data for years before 1980 are estimated by trending backwards using alternative data on total employment (domestic concept) from the EC's AMECO Database.
	United Kingdom	Data missing in the OECD National Accounts Database for years before 1980. Data for years before 1980 are estimated by trending backwards using alternative data on total employment (domestic concept) from the EC's AMECO Database
Hours worked for total employment	Canada	Data missing in the OECD National Accounts Database for years before 1997. Data for years before 1997 are estimated by trending backwards using data on annual hours worked per worker from the OECD Employment Database.
	Finland	Data missing in the OECD National Accounts Database for years before 1975. Data for years before 1975 are estimated by trending backwards using data on annual hours worked per worker from the OECD Employment Database.
	Iceland	Data fully missing in the OECD National Accounts Database for all years. Replaced with estimates based on data on annual hours worked per worker from the OECD Employment Database.
	Japan	No data on hours worked for total employment in the OECD National Accounts Database
	Norway	All data refer to mainland employment only (i.e. excluding oil and gas). Data are taken from Statistics Norway.
	United Kingdom	Data missing in the OECD National Accounts Database for years before 1994. Data for years before 1994 are estimated by trending backwards using data on annual hours worked per worker from the OECD Employment Database.
	United States	Data missing in the OECD National Accounts Database for years before 1998. Data for years before 1998 are estimated by trending backwards using data on annual hours worked per worker from the OECD Employment Database
Population by age and gender	Canada	Data missing in the OECD Employment Database for years before 1976. Data for years before 1976 are estimated by trending backwards using alternative data on population by gender from Statistics Canada. Estimates produced for all ages and 15-64 year-olds only.
	Denmark	Data missing in the OECD Employment Database for years before 1983. Data for years before 1983 are estimated by trending backwards using alternative data on population by gender from Eurostat. Estimates produced for all ages and 15-64 year-olds only.
	Iceland	Data missing in the OECD Employment Database for years before 1991. Data for years before 1991 are estimated by trending backwards using alternative data on population by gender from Iceland.
	United Kingdom	Data missing in the OECD Employment Database for years before 1984. Data for years before 1984 are estimated by trending backwards using alternative data on population by age and gender from Eurostat. Estimates produced for all ages and 15-64 year-olds only.
Employment by age and gender	Canada	Data missing in the OECD Employment Database for years before 1976. Data for years before 1976 are estimated by trending backwards using alternative data on employment by gender from the OECD Annual Labour Force Statistics Database. Estimates produced for all ages and 15-64 year-olds only.
	Denmark	Data missing in the OECD Employment Database for years before 1976. Data for years before 1983 are estimated by trending backwards using alternative data on employment by gender from the OECD Annual Labour Force Statistics Database. Estimates produced for all ages and 15-64 year-olds only.
	France	Data missing in the OECD Employment Database for years before 1968. Data for years before 1968 are estimated by trending backwards using alternative data on employment by gender from the OECD Annual Labour Force Statistics Database. Estimates produced for all ages and 15-64 year-olds only.

	Iceland	Data missing in the OECD Employment Database for years before 1991. Data for years before 1991 are estimated by trending backwards using alternative data on labour force participation and unemployment from the Icelandic Census and national estimates of employment derived from accident insurance records and provided to the OECD by the National Economic Institute of Iceland.
	United Kingdom	Data missing in the OECD Employment Database for years before 1984. Data for years before 1984 are estimated by trending backwards using alternative data on employment by gender from the OECD Annual Labour Force Statistics Database. Estimates produced for all ages and 15-64 year-olds only.
Average usual weekly working hours by age and gender	Canada	Data fully missing in the OECD Employment Database. Replaced with alternative data on average usual weekly working hours by age and gender from Statistics Canada.
	Finland	Data missing in the OECD Employment Database for years before 2001. Data for years before 2001 are estimated by trending backwards using alternative data on working hours (average annual hours actually worked) provided by Statistics Finland. Estimates produced for all ages only.
	Iceland	Data missing in the OECD Employment Database for years before 2000. Data for years before 2000 are estimated by trending backwards using alternative data on working hours (average actual working hours) provided by Statistics Iceland. Estimates produced for all ages only.
	Italy	Data missing in the OECD Employment Database for years before 1995. Data for years before 1995 are estimated by trending backwards using alternative data on average usual weekly working hours from Eurostat. Estimates produced for all ages only.
	Norway	Data missing in the OECD Employment Database for years before 1996. Data for years before 1996 are estimated by trending backwards using alternative data on working hours (average actual weekly working hours) from Statistics Norway. Estimates produced for all ages only
	Sweden	Data missing in the OECD Employment Database for years before 2002. Data for years before 2002 are estimated by trending backwards using alternative data on average usual weekly working hours provided by Statistics Sweden. Estimates produced for all ages only
	United States	Data refer to average hours for dependent employees only.

Development accounting estimates in Section 3.3

The analysis presented in Section 3.3 is based on development accounting – a procedure similar to the growth accounting technique discussed above, but used to identify and decompose the sources of differences in economic output across economies, rather than growth within a single economy over time. The principle in this case is to use macroeconomic data to split differences in output into parts accounted for by differences in labour, in capital, and in total factor productivity. As with growth accounting, data permitting, the contributions of each of these main components can then be decomposed further into their own sub-components.

Theoretical model

The theoretical framework used for the development accounting exercise is analogous to that used for the growth accounting exercise above. Using the standard Cobb-Douglas production function outlined above and based on the re-arranged model shown in equation 4, relative differences in GDP per capita between two economies (A and B) at a given point in time can be expressed using the following multiplicative function:

$$\frac{\frac{Y_A}{P_A}}{\frac{Y_B}{P_B}} = \frac{\left(\frac{Y_A}{E_A.H_A}\right)}{\left(\frac{Y_B}{E_B.H_B}\right)} \cdot \frac{\left(\frac{WP_A}{P_A}\right)}{\left(\frac{WP_B}{P_B}\right)} \cdot \frac{\left(\frac{E_A}{WP_A}\right)}{\left(\frac{E_B}{WP_B}\right)} \cdot \frac{\left(\frac{H_A}{E_A}\right)}{\left(\frac{H_B}{E_B}\right)} \tag{11}$$

where A is the economy of interest, and B is a benchmark economy chosen to provide a point of comparison. The choice of benchmark economy is largely arbitrary, though different choices can alter the ease of interpretation. In the results shown in Section 3.3, the OECD total is chosen as the benchmark 'economy'. Results therefore show the relative gap in GDP per capita between a given economy and the OECD as a whole and the factors that contribute to the relative gap in GDP per capita between a given economy and the OECD as a whole.

Relative differences in the employment rate (E/WP) and hours worked per person employed (H/E) can then be further decomposed using the following two additive functions based on equations 5 and 6:

$$(12)$$

$$\frac{\left(\frac{E_A}{WP_A}\right)}{\left(\frac{E_B}{WP_B}\right)} = \frac{\left(\frac{E_{(15-24)men_A}}{WP_A}\right)}{\left(\frac{E_{(15-24)men_B}}{WP_B}\right)} + \frac{\left(\frac{E_{(15-24)women_A}}{WP_A}\right)}{\left(\frac{E_{(15-24)women_B}}{WP_B}\right)} + \frac{\left(\frac{E_{(25-54)men_A}}{WP_A}\right)}{\left(\frac{E_{(25-54)men_B}}{WP_B}\right)} + \frac{\left(\frac{E_{(25-54)women_A}}{WP_A}\right)}{\left(\frac{E_{(25-54)women_B}}{WP_B}\right)} + $$

$$\frac{\left(\frac{E_{(55-64)men_A}}{WP_A}\right)}{\left(\frac{E_{(55-64)men_B}}{WP_B}\right)} + \frac{\left(\frac{E_{(55-64)women_A}}{WP_A}\right)}{\left(\frac{E_{(55-64)women_B}}{WP_B}\right)}$$

And

$$(13)$$

$$\frac{\left(\frac{H}{WP_A}\right)}{\left(\frac{H_B}{E_B}\right)} = \frac{\left(\frac{H_{(15-24)men_A}}{E_A}\right)}{\left(\frac{H_{(15-24)men_B}}{E_B}\right)} + \frac{\left(\frac{H_{(15-24)women_A}}{E_A}\right)}{\left(\frac{H_{(15-24)women_B}}{E_B}\right)} + \frac{\left(\frac{H_{(25-54)men_A}}{E_A}\right)}{\left(\frac{H_{(25-54)men_B}}{E_B}\right)} + \frac{\left(\frac{H_{(25-54)women_A}}{E_A}\right)}{\left(\frac{H_{(25-54)women_B}}{E_B}\right)} + $$

$$\frac{\left(\frac{H_{(55-64)men_A}}{E_A}\right)}{\left(\frac{H_{(55-64)men_B}}{E_B}\right)} + \frac{\left(\frac{H_{(55-64)women_A}}{E_A}\right)}{\left(\frac{H_{(55-64)women_B}}{E_B}\right)}$$

These three equations (11-13) form the core of the development accounting exercise.

Data and estimation procedure

Estimation itself is again conducted using the Shapley decomposition (Shorrocks, 2013[93]). It is again run separately for each country, and once more takes place in two stages. First, the relative difference in GDP per capita between the given country and the OECD total is decomposed into each of its main components – as shown in equation 11 above, into the contributions of differences in labour productivity (Y/(E.H)), in the working age share of the population (WP/P), in the employment rate (E/WP), and in average hours worked per person employed (H.E). Second, the contributions of relative differences in both the employment-to-population rate (E/WP) and in average hours worked per person employed (H.E) are then themselves decomposed by gender and age-group, as shown in equations 12 and 13. Again, it is these last two decompositions that are of primary interest – they estimate the contribution of the relative level of men's and women's employment and working hours to any gap in GDP per capita between the given country and the OECD as a whole.

As with the growth accounting exercise, the data used are based on combination of official macro-economic data from national accounts databases and employment and working hours estimates from labour force surveys. More specifically, data for the first stage are taken from the *OECD National Accounts Database* (Table A B.1), while data for the second stage are estimated using information from labour force surveys, in the same way as above. The labour force survey data themselves are taken primarily from the *OECD Employment Database* (Table A B.1). Because the development accounting exercise is run just for the latest year available (2015), there are far fewer problems here with missing data. On the few occasions that data are missing, data points are filled using the same steps as outlined above (see Table A B.2).

It is worth noting here that complete national accounts data is currently available for only 30 OECD member countries. The exceptions are Chile, Iceland, Japan, Mexico and Turkey, all of whom are missing information on one or more key measures in the *OECD National Accounts Database*. As a result, the OECD 'total' used as the reference economy for the development accounting exercise refers to OECD-30 total (that is, the weighted total across the remaining 30 OECD member countries), only.

Forward-looking labour force and GDP per capita projections in Section 4

The forward looking projections presented in Section 4 are produced based on a combination of estimates from the OECD's in-house labour force projection model – a dynamic age-cohort model that estimates labour participation up to the year 2060 – and a modified version of the OECD's long-term growth models (as presented in OECD (2014[92]), *OECD Economic Outlook No. 95*). The projections look to model the impact of a range of different 'gender gap' scenarios, each of which assumes a different trajectory for gender differences in labour force participation and working hours:

- The *baseline* scenario, where labour force participation rates of men and women (15-74) are estimated using the OECD's standard dynamic age-cohort model, which projects participation rates (by gender and five-year age-groups) based on current (2007-16) rates of labour market entry and exit, and average usual weekly working hours for each gender and five year age group are held constant at their 2016 values. This scenario services as our reference or baseline scenario.
- *Scenario A: gender participation gaps reduced by 25% by 2025 and by 50% in 2040.* In this scenario, male participation rates are held at the baseline and female participation rates are projected so that the gender participation gap observed in 2012 within each five-year age-group falls by 25% by 2025, and 50% by 2040. This scenario incorporates the G20 "25% by 2025" target. Average usual weekly working hours are held at the baseline.
- *Scenario B: gender participation gaps reduced by 50% by 2025 and 100% by 2040.* In this scenario, male participation rates are held at the baseline and female rates are projected so that the gender participation gap observed in 2012 within each five-year age group falls by 50% by 2025, and 100% (i.e. is fully closed) by 2040. Average usual weekly working hours are held at the baseline.
- *Scenario C: gender participation gaps and gender working hours gaps reduced by 25% by 2025 and by 50% by 2040, with women increasing working hours.* This scenario assumes that gender gaps in both labour force participation rates and usual weekly working hours decline for each five-year age-group by 25% by 2025 and 50% by 2040, with the gender working hours gap closed entirely through increases in *female* working hours (male hours follow the baseline).
- *Scenario D: gender participation gaps and gender working hours gaps reduced by 25% by 2025 and by 50% by 2040, with men decreasing working hours.* This scenario is the same as scenario C, but gender working hours gaps closed entirely through decreases in male hours, rather than increases in female hours. Female hours follow the baseline.
- *Scenario E: gender participation gaps and gender working hours gaps reduced by 50% by 2025 and by 100% by 2040, with women increasing working hours.* This is a "full convergence" scenario. It assumes that gender gaps in both labour

force participation rates and usual weekly working hours decline for each five-year age-group by 50% by 2025 and 100% (i.e. are fully closed) by 2040, with the gender working hours gap closed entirely through increases in *female* working hours (male hours follow the baseline trend).

Production of the estimates themselves takes place in two stages. First, estimates of the size of the labour force and overall average working hours under each scenario are produced by applying the assumed labour participation rates and working hours to the OECD's in-house labour force projection model. The model is a dynamic age-cohort model that, under baseline conditions, projects future labour participation by gender and five-year age-group using current rates of labour market entry and exit. For the various hypothetical 'gender gap' scenarios, participation rates and, where needed, working hours for the relevant gender and age-groups are forced so that they meet the given assumed gender gap targets by the given target year. Adjustment is assumed to occur linearly between the projection start year (2017) and the target year. The resulting estimates are then summed across both genders and all five-year age groups to produce estimates of the size of the overall labour force (15-74 year-olds – see below) and overall average working hours.

Second, estimates of GDP per capita and GDP per capita growth under each scenario are produced by combining the labour force and working hours estimates with a modified version of the long-term growth models presented by the OECD in OECD Economic Outlook No. 95 (see Johansson et al. (2013[89]) for technical details). The theoretical foundation for the long-term growth models is similar to that outlined for the growth accounting exercise above. The models estimate GDP based on a standard Cobb-Douglas production function, with the usual long-term growth determinants (i.e. labour, physical capital, human capital and total factor productivity). Potential GDP across the projection period (here, 2012 to 2040) is estimated by projecting trends and changes in the various input components, with projections of the components themselves based on both long-term dynamics within the given country and on convergence patterns between countries (see OECD (2014[92]) and Johansson et al. (2013[89]) for details on the measures, data and assumptions used to project the individual components).

Potential GDP per capita and GDP per capita growth under each scenario is estimated by adjusting projections from these long-term growth models according to the assumed change (relative to the baseline) in the overall labour force participation rate and the assumed change (relative to the baseline) in overall average usual weekly working hours. No change is assumed in the baseline scenario, so the estimates of GDP per capita in this scenario are identical to those in the OECD Economic Outlook No. 95. In each case changes and developments in all other production factors – such as physical capital and human capital and the remaining sub components of potential employment and labour efficiency – are held steady at the baseline.

It should be pointed out that the projections used in these scenarios are simply mechanical. In other words, they assume that any changes in labour force participation rates or weekly working hours do not interact with, or have any indirect effects on, other labour inputs or any other production factors, including physical or human capital. It is possible, for example, that changes in labour force participation rates and weekly working hours among, say, parenting-age women (25-54 year-olds) could lead to changes in participation and/or hours among older workers if, for instance, grandparents or older friends and relatives are used as substitute carers for children. If any such indirect effects occur, the impact of changes in patterns of paid work on the overall labour supply may differ from those estimated here. It should also be noted that, just as with the growth accounting estimates presented in Section 3, the projections do not factor in any possible effects of changes in patterns of paid work on household production. Again, to the extent that changes in male or female labour supply lead to changes in household production or to shifts between measured and unmeasured economic activity, the estimates shown here may not fully capture the effects of a change in patterns of paid work on economic output.

Lastly, as touched on at the start of Section 4, it is worth pointing out that the measures and units used for these forward-looking projections differ slightly from those used in Section 3. Specifically, while Section 3 concentrates on employment rates and a 15-64 year-old age group, here estimates are based on labour force participation rates (i.e. the employed plus unemployed population) and a 15-74 year-old age group. This is to help ensure compatibility with the inputs used for the OECD's standard long-term growth models – which use labour participation as a core input, and the age-group 15-74 (OECD, 2014[92]) – and because the participation of over-65 workers is likely to increase in importance in future decades.

Notes

[1] Because of potential behavioural responses, of other economic actors, we cannot be certain about what the Nordic economies would have looked like if female employment had not grown over the previous few decades – it is possible those women already in employment might have adjusted their working hours to compensate, for instance, or perhaps men in employment might have reacted differently.

[2] The socio-economic systems of the Åland Islands, the Faroe Islands and Greenland are based on the same factors as the rest of the Nordic Countries. The welfare system is financed through taxation (including social security contributions) and is universal; the labour market model is based on the same collaborative principles as in the other Nordic countries; and policy development has a strong equality focus with policy supports that include parental leave and subsidized childcare. However, there are certain characteristics of the labour markets and types of jobs in these countries that differentiate them from, for instance, Denmark, Norway and Sweden.

[3] In Finland, the quota applied only to fathers. It took the form of a bonus, where fathers were entitled to two extra weeks of paid leave if they took two weeks of the sharable parental leave. This was later extended to four week and then, in 2013, simplified into a nine-week non-transferable fathers-only paid leave, of which up to 18 days can be taken while the mother is on maternity or parental leave.

[4] For Norway, this estimate is slightly higher than a similar estimate produced by Østbakken (2016[15]), who found that roughly 0.20 percentage points of average annual GDP per capita growth over the period 1972-2013 can be linked to changes in female employment. There are several differences in methods and data between the two studies. For example, unlike this study Østbakken (2016[15]), included men's and women's hourly wages as measures of male and female productivity. Given that women's hourly wages have historically been (and still are) lower than men's on average, this is likely to produce smaller estimates of the contribution of changes in women's employment, *ceteris paribus*.

[5] For both Denmark and Iceland, for example, the time period covered in Figure 3.3 is shorter than the period covered in Figure 3.1 and Figure 3.2.

ORGANISATION FOR ECONOMIC CO-OPERATION AND DEVELOPMENT

The OECD is a unique forum where governments work together to address the economic, social and environmental challenges of globalisation. The OECD is also at the forefront of efforts to understand and to help governments respond to new developments and concerns, such as corporate governance, the information economy and the challenges of an ageing population. The Organisation provides a setting where governments can compare policy experiences, seek answers to common problems, identify good practice and work to co-ordinate domestic and international policies.

The OECD member countries are: Australia, Austria, Belgium, Canada, Chile, the Czech Republic, Denmark, Estonia, Finland, France, Germany, Greece, Hungary, Iceland, Ireland, Israel, Italy, Japan, Korea, Latvia, Luxembourg, Mexico, the Netherlands, New Zealand, Norway, Poland, Portugal, the Slovak Republic, Slovenia, Spain, Sweden, Switzerland, Turkey, the United Kingdom and the United States. The European Union takes part in the work of the OECD.

OECD Publishing disseminates widely the results of the Organisation's statistics gathering and research on economic, social and environmental issues, as well as the conventions, guidelines and standards agreed by its members.

OECD PUBLISHING, 2, rue André-Pascal, 75775 PARIS CEDEX 16
(81 2018 11 1 P) ISBN 978-92-64-30003-3 – 2018